EIR (ISSN 0273-6314) *is published weekly
(50 issues), by EIR News Service, Inc.,
P.O. Box 17390, Washington, D.C. 20041-0390.
(703) 777-9451 ext. 415*

***European Headquarters:*** E.I.R. GmbH, Postfach
Bahnstrasse 9a, D-65205, Wiesbaden, Germany
Tel: 49-611-73650
Homepage: http://www.eirna.com
e-mail: eirna@eirna.com
Director: Georg Neudecker

***Montreal, Canada:*** 514-461-1557

***Denmark:*** EIR - Danmark, Sankt Knuds Vej 11,
basement left, DK-1903 Frederiksberg, Denmark.
Tel.: +45 35 43 60 40, Fax: +45 35 43 87 57. e-mail:
eirdk@hotmail.com.

***Mexico City:*** EIR, Sor Juana Inés de la Cruz 242-2
Col. Agricultura C.P. 11360
Delegación M. Hidalgo, México D.F.
Tel. (5525) 5318-2301
eirmexico@gmail.com

# *Perfide Albion*

## EDITORIAL

# British Coup Against U.S. Presidency Begins to Crumble

### by Rachel Brown

March 12—As Lyndon LaRouche said this week: "The British *are* the media, with the intention to ruin nations. It's been done before, and is being attempted again. Watch out."

It is clear that there is an intention to disrupt and destroy the Trump presidency from the highest levels of the British oligarchy. The U.S.-Russia-China alliance now in the early stage of formation will end London-centered imperial geopolitics, and set out a new era of mutually beneficial cooperation among nations. The thrust of the last two British-loyal presidencies of Bush and Obama has been voted out. The British Empire is about to go out of existence.

A survey of recent "news" reports published both before and after President Trump's inauguration, show the British attempt to topple the current U.S. presidency is in full force. Take for example just a few of the significant accusations and their origination:

- January 10, 2017—*Buzzfeed News* releases a 35 page dossier on Trump's alleged collusion with Russia, containing numerous refutable allegations and anonymous sources. It later comes out

Flickr/Gage Skidmore

*Donald Trump speaking with the media at a hangar at Mesa Gateway Airport in Mesa, Arizona, Feb. 8, 2017.*

that the author of the dossier was Christopher Steele, a former MI6 agent. The document was alleged to have been requested by political opponents of Trump in the United States, first on the Republican side, then by Democrats.

- January 12, 2017—A BBC article by Paul Wood initiates the concept of Trump as a Russian agent, claiming to have four sources, all unnamed, who confirm the validity of the assertions in the dossier. He sets up the impeachment tone, "It is an extraordinary situation, ten days before Mr. Trump is sworn into office, but it was foreshadowed during the campaign." The article presents no evidence, in fact even admitting that no financial traces or video evidence were found, however it concludes by quoting former CIA director Michael Morell and former CIA and NSA head Michael Hayden, calling Trump "an unwitting agent of the Russian Federation," and "a useful fool." The BBC's Wood states, "Agent; puppet—both terms imply some measure of influence or control by Moscow... The background to those statements was information held—at the time—within the intelligence community. Now all Americans have heard the claims. Little more than a week before his inauguration, they will have to decide if their president-elect really was being blackmailed by Moscow."

- January 19, 2017—George Soros, during an interview at the World Economic Forum in Davos, Switzerland, "predicts" the Trump presidency will not succeed, and that disunity, of which he is a leading purveyor, will prevail, saying, "I personally am convinced that he is going to fail... not because of people like me who would like him to fail, but because his ideas that guide him are inherently self-contradictory and the contradictions are already embodied by his advisors."

- January 21, 2017—A *Spectator* article, by the same Paul Wood, is published, entitled, "Will Donald Trump be assassinated, ousted in a coup or just impeached?" It quotes Alexander Hamilton, about "the desire in foreign powers to gain an improper ascendant in our councils," and claims again that Trump is a Russian "agent of influence," bought or blackmailed by the Kremlin. The title of the article speaks for itself. It then introduces the emoluments allegation as cause for impeachment, concluding, "Impeachment—however far-fetched an idea—is not the most outlandish possibility being discussed in this town as the 45th president is sworn into office."

- January 23, 2017—Citizens for Responsible Ethics (CREW), files emoluments lawsuit against President Trump in New York Southern District Court. CREW is a George Soros-funded organization, having received $740,000 from the Soros family Foundation to Promote Open Society since 2010, and another $150,000 from the Open Society Institute in 2010. The current chairman of CREW, David Brock, is not new to British-run coups against U.S. Presidents. He also initiated the media campaign "Troopergate," as a writer for the conservative magazine *American Spectator* in 1994, which led to the impeachment of Democratic President Clinton. Brock has not changed sides, but is merely continuing his work on behalf of the British Empire.

- March 2, 2017—The *Independent* of London reports that members of the U.S. Congress, despite the Steele dossier having been exposed as absurd and full of errors, are seeking Steele's testimony in the upcoming Congressional investigation of Trump's ties to Russia. The *Independent* states, "it is understood Democrats—as well as some Republicans—in Congress are prepared to facilitate discreet initial meetings in the UK or on other neutral territory." It also is widely reported that the FBI sought to pay Steele to continue his investigation, even after the intelligence was discredited.

## The Counterattack

The transparent fraud, British sponsorship, and absurd lies that have been circulated concerning President Trump are now beginning to backfire against the conspirators who wish to overthrow the duly elected Trump and be rid of his Presidency.

Sen. Chuck Grassley, Chairperson of the Senate Intelligence Committee, stated in a letter to James Comey, head of the FBI, "The idea that the FBI and associates of the Clinton campaign would pay Mr. Steele to investigate the Republican nominee for President in the run-up to the election raises substantial questions about the FBI's independence from politics, as well as the Obama administration's use of law enforcement and intelligence agencies for political ends... It is additionally troubling that the FBI reportedly agreed to such an arrangement given that, in January of 2017, [former Director of National Intelligence] James Clapper issued a statement stating that 'the [intelligence community] has not made any judgment that the information in this document is reliable, and we did not rely upon it in any way for our conclusions.'"

In recent days the Trump administration has turned the tables on the attempted coup, accusing the Obama administration of wiretapping Trump Tower before the election, an investigation of which will likely lead to full exposure of the British-run nature of the coup. Numerous reports point to British intelligence playing a key role in the wiretapping and intelligence gathering.

Lawrence Wilkerson, former chief of staff to Colin Powell, speaking on his "Wilkerson Report" radio show, was asked about Trump's wiretapping allegations. He responded, "Well, I'm certainly not one to defend HMS Trump and that whole entourage of people, but I will paint you a hypothetical here. There are a number of events that have occurred in the last 96 hours or so that lead me to believe that maybe even the Democratic party—whatever element of it—approached John Brennan at the CIA, maybe even the former president of the United States. And John Brennan, not wanting his fingerprints to be on anything, went to his colleague in London GCHQ, MI6, and essentially said, `Give me anything you've got.' And he got something and he turned it over to the DNC or to someone like that. And what he got was GCHQ MI6's tapes of conversations of the Trump administration, perhaps even the President himself. It's really kind of strange, at least to me, they let the head of that organization [Britain's GCHQ] go, fired him about the same time this was brewing up. So I'm not one to defend Trump, but in this case *he might be right.* It's just that it wasn't the FBI. Comey's right, he wasn't wire-tapping anybody, it was John Brennan, at the CIA."

Larry Johnson, former CIA analyst, wrote in his blog "No Quarter," that at least some of the "intercepted communications" of Trump aides reported in the *New York Times* on Jan. 20th, "were done by foreign entities and that this was done *with the knowledge of Obama administration officials.*" Johnson then discusses the arrangement between the NSA and the British spy agency, GCHQ, whereby under standard operating procedure, GCHQ intercepts communications in a way that would be illegal for a U.S. agency to do under U.S. law, and then passes these on to U.S. intelligence officials. (*EIR* exposed this program years ago, including when Edward Snowden first exploded the NSA scandal, and when the Democrats opposed such police state measures.) Johnson also stresses the very public assertions, as in the *New York Times* article of March 1, that President Obama moved in the last phases of his presidency, to loosen intelligence secrecy provisions so that "information" about alleged links between the Trump administration and the Russians could be available to a wide array of individuals, and to European allies.

*Newsweek* reported, on February 15, that NATO countries, under British direction, were engaged in widespread intelligence collection on Trump campaign and administration officials. Author Kurt Eichenwald wrote, "The Western European intelligence operations began in August, after the British government obtained information that people acting on behalf of Russia were in contact with members of the Trump campaign. Those details from the British were widely shared among the NATO allies in Europe." His sources reported surveillance, ranging from intercepting telephone calls to gathering electronic and human source information.

The truth of the British role—as well as the personal law-breaking of Barack Obama—is now surfacing. Perhaps the destruction which they were plotting will, in the end, be their own.

# EIR Contents

www.larouchepub.com Volume 44, Number 11, March 17, 2017

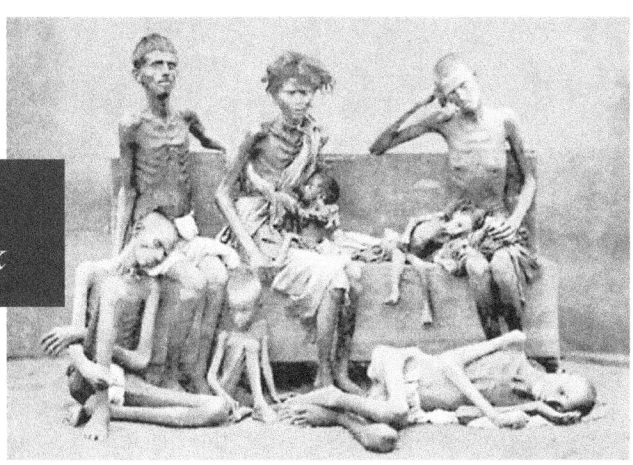

**Cover This Week**

Churchill's Bengali famine of 1943 (See page 13)

# I. New Opportunities

FRANKFURT, GERMANY

# LaRouche Associate Addresses Forum On the 'Coup' Against Donald Trump

by Dean Andromidas

March 8—Harley Schlanger, a close collaborator of American economist Lyndon LaRouche for many years, addressed yesterday an audience of some 100 businessmen and German reserve officers in Frankfurt, Germany, on the British-orchestrated coup against U.S. President Donald Trump. The event was organized jointly by the Landesfachkommission Internationaler Kreis des Wirtschaftsrats Hessen, a business association associated with the CDU, and the Reservistenkameradschaft Frankfurt am Main, on the theme "Who Is

Out To Sabotage the 'Trump Revolution' and Why?" Schlanger was the guest speaker at the event which was attended by 100 guests, half of them in uniform.

In his introduction, Lt. Col. (Res.) Axel Ebbecke welcomed many of the more prominent guests, including "a special guest, Mrs. Helga Zepp-LaRouche, President of the Schiller Institute, whose husband, Mr. Lyndon LaRouche, is well-known in the United States for his presidential campaigns and the fact that he served as an advisor to the Ronald Reagan Administra-

Reservistenkameradschaft Frankfurt/Maria Bürkle

*Harley Schlanger addresses the forum in Frankfurt.*

The British-orchestrated and George Soros-financed coup effort against President Trump, carried out by the same networks that had launched the coup against the elected government of Ukraine in 2014 ... Trump's election was part of a global rejection of the policies of the last twenty years—including the permanent war doctrine and the neo-liberal economic policy of globalization.

tion on the policy of the Strategic Defense Initiative." Schlanger was introduced with a brief review of his background, including that he had been Mr. LaRouche's official spokesman and bureau chief of *EIR* in the Southwest of the United States.

Schlanger gave a very hard-hitting presentation detailing the British-orchestrated and George Soros-financed coup effort against President Trump, carried out by the same networks that had launched the coup against the elected government of Ukraine in 2014. He further explained that Trump's election was part of a global rejection of the policies of the last twenty years—including the permanent war doctrine and the neo-liberal economic policy of globalization—many of which Trump committed himself to reversing.

Schlanger especially elaborated on Trump's intention to establish a positive relationship with the leaders of both Russia and China to reverse the Obama/British-led drive for World War III. In this context, he went into the cause of the ongoing financial crisis, the need to re-enact the Glass-Steagall Act and LaRouche's Four Laws, as well as the need for the U.S. and Europe to join China, Russia, and the BRICS in China's Belt and Road Initiative.

Many of the guests indicated their agreement with a number of the points, including on the coup in Ukraine and the futility of sanctions against Russia.

The presentation was followed by a lively Q&A. One question which reflected what many were thinking, came from a television journalist, who brought up his theory as to why the German media give such biased coverage to Trump: "Do you think the Germans need an image of an evil enemy so they will accept the status quo? I am astonished that the coverage is so nasty."

Schlanger used his response to elaborate on what he had said earlier about the brainwashing of the Germans around "collective guilt" over World War II. He spoke of the role of the Bush-Harriman networks in installing the Nazis, and

said it is time for Germany to break free of this, which is part of a continuing occupation of Germany. Many people approached him afterwards to thank him for that, with one noting that "we, as Germans, are afraid to tell the truth—it is good you did so!"

One business professor questioned whether Bush and Obama were really responsible for the lack of good jobs, indicating that the problem is robotics and smart technologies, and that it will just get worse. In his reply, Schlanger discussed how the Chinese are creating productive jobs, with the Belt and Road Initiative, which will continue to produce jobs, because of the emphasis on science in the economy. New scientific discovery is an opportunity to inspire youth for the future, he underscored, rather than something which means a larger pool of a permanent unemployable class.

One guest thanked Schlanger for his presentation, which reflected a deep understanding of American politics, adding: "Perhaps you can help us and tell us what is wrong with Chancellor Angela Merkel?"

EIRNS/Sylvia Spaniolo

*On Feb. 23, the third anniversary of the coup against Ukraine, LaRouche PAC organized an International Day of Action and released a dossier— "Obama and Soros Color Revolutions: Nazis in Ukraine, 2014; USA, 2017?" Above, LaRouche PAC organizer Diane Sare in Manhattan. See EIR, Feb. 24, 2017.*

# *EIR* Editor Testifies on Glass-Steagall Before the Maryland Legislature

*Testimony of Paul Gallagher,* EIR *Economics Co-Editor, March 3, 2017, before the Ways and Means Committee of the Maryland House of Delegates, on a resolution to move the U.S. Congress to restore the Glass-Steagall Act, Maryland House Resolution HJ4.*

Committee Chair and Delegates,

Thank you very much for holding today's hearing on the resolution to the U.S. Congress to restore the Glass-Steagall Act separating commercial bank units from all other types of financial institutions, and limiting FDIC insurance to those units.

Glass-Steagall restoration legislation in the U.S. House of Representatives, H.R.790, the Return to Prudent Banking Act of 2017, was introduced Feb. 1 by Republican Walter Jones of North Carolina, and Democrats Marcy Kaptur and Tim Ryan of Ohio and Tulsi Gabbard of Hawaii. It has grown to 32 [now 37] co-sponsors, and needs support. Twelve state legislatures are now considering resolutions supporting this legislation.

If Glass-Steagall is not restored now, the next large bank—or non-bank—financial failure will again topple the banking system and trigger both new bailouts and confiscation of bondholders and depositors in the form of bail-in. U.S.-based large bank holding companies have $2 trillion in exposure to European megabanks, which are full of non-performing loans and have not had a single profitable year since the 2008 crash, despite hundreds of billions in bailouts and trillions in bond purchases by the European Central Bank.

And if Glass-Steagall separation is not restored now, the largest U.S. bank holding companies—which dominate the banking system to the extent of 60-70% of deposits and assets—will continue to limit lending, in practice, to the large corporate bond issuers and borrowers, shutting out technologically progressive SMEs from credit.

JPMorgan Chase had $837 billion in loans/leases outstanding at Dec. 31, 2015, just 65.1% of its deposits of $1.279 trillion. Citigroup had $605 billion in loans/leases at the same date, just 66.8% of its deposits. But the entire U.S. commercial banking system has loans/leases outstanding equal to 79.2% of deposits according to the Federal Reserve's flow-of-funds report. Since the six largest banks hold more than half of all deposits, the comparative ratio for the nation's 6,000 community banks and regionals clearly must be in the range of 90%-plus loans/leases to deposits. The biggest banks' loan ratios are very low indeed; they both hurt the economy and demonstrate the great degree to which households' and businesses' deposits are being used for securities and derivatives speculation.

But since the 2008 crash, the biggest 12 banks have largely absorbed the deposits and assets of some 2,000 small banks that have disappeared—one quarter of all the commercial banks which existed in the United States a decade ago.

The largest bank holding companies changed dramatically from 1995—the point at which Glass-Steagall enforcement had effectively ceased—through the 2007-08 crash. This was studied and effectively described already in a 2011 study by the New York Federal Reserve entitled, "Peeling the Onion: The Structure of Large Bank Holding Companies." These giants became impossibly complex, morphing from 100-200 subsidiaries typically in 1995 to 3,000 or more units per megabank in 2011. They became giants dominating the assets and deposits of the entire U.S. banking system for the first time in U.S. history. They shifted their huge and growing deposit bases from lending toward supporting securities trading units, derivatives trades, etc.

Creative Commons/*Maryland Reporter*

EIR *Economics Co-Editor Paul Gallagher testified before the Ways and Means Committee of the Maryland House of Delegates, March 3, 2017.*

Derivatives markets exploded ten times in size in ten years 1997-2007.

Already in 1998-99, the failure of a single hedge fund called Long Term Capital Management was admitted to have nearly caused a global bank panic, because 55 U.S. and European banks, through leveraged loans, were into LTCM's immensely risky derivatives trading. By 2008, Lehman Brothers and other investment banks, insurance companies, and hedge funds were in the same blowout event condition.

Today, a media report March 2 identified $321 billion in fines which the world's biggest banks have had to pay since the 2008 crash, for illegal and/or immoral activities which they continue to commit up to the present. The dominant character of these violations of banking law and practice is the use of the very large deposit bases of these banks to support speculative units, securitization of investments, and derivatives bets. The currently very public Wells Fargo mis-selling scandal is emblematic of this.

## To Restore Commercial Lending

If the Glass-Steagall Act *is* restored by Congress now, financial failures will take down only individual financial institutions, as when important investment banks like Drexel Burnham Lambert and Solomon Brothers failed under Glass-Steagall enforcement without affecting the rest of the banking system. U.S. branches of the biggest European universal banks, which absorbed great volumes of taxpayer bailout loans and recapitalizations, will have to recharter themselves completely independently if they are to operate in the United States at all. But in fact, Glass-Steagall restoration in the United States is likely to be followed more or less immediately in Europe, where many nations have already had Glass-Steagall bank separation legislation introduced.

And if Glass-Steagall *is* restored by Congress now, even as large holding companies are divesting securities units, their commercial banking units will necessarily be in the business of lending to businesses and households, aside from holdings of Federal and municipal bonds. The common Wall Street argument against Glass-Steagall—that it will reduce bank lending or damage the capital market—is the opposite of the truth. As FDIC vice-chair Thomas Hoenig has frequently argued in recent years, the United States capital markets were the deepest and most reliable in the world in the decades when commercial banking and securities trading were separated and the Federal safety net protected only the former.

If a national bank for great infrastructure projects is established, it will need a system of private commercial banks lending on good terms to its contractors. Glass-Steagall will again make lending the business of those banks.

*EIR* believes that restoring Glass-Steagall is the initiating action of four laws Congress should take. It should lead to a national Hamiltonian credit institutions for trillions in infrastructure investments; to an accelerated return to manned space exploration and to rapid development of fusion power and plasma technologies.

Thank you again for debating this crucial subject.

# II. *Perfide Albion*

# Hack Attack: Pearl Harbor or Watergate?
# A Right to Control the Narrative, or Truth?

by Helga Zepp-LaRouche, chair of the German political party
Civil Rights Movement Solidarity (BüSo)

March 11—Six weeks after President Trump took office, the neoliberal Establishment has still not reconciled itself with the results of the United States' democratic election. The neoliberal, globalist mainstream media are in a head-over-heels, non-stop campaign, claiming that Russian hacking attacks helped Trump to win.

In reality, something entirely different is going on: First, Trump has promised and is determined to end the British imperial policy of endless war in the Middle East, and instead to put the U.S. relationship with Russia and China on a rational basis. And second, this whole campaign is occurring against a backdrop in which the trans-Atlantic financial system could implode at any minute, and in which Trump, according to his press spokesman Sean Spicer, is sticking to his intention to institute the Glass-Steagall system of bank separation, which is a red flag for the City of London and Wall Street.

The *Washington Post* and *New York Times* repeat daily the "narrative" of the alleged Russia-gate, and *New York Times* columnist Thomas L. Friedman has even brought out the big guns and compared the alleged

National Security
## Declassified report says Putin 'ordered' effort to undermine faith in U.S. election and help Trump

Sessions did not disclose meetings with Russian ambassador

By Evan Perez, Shimon Prokupecz and Eli Watkins, CNN
Updated 3:40 PM ET, Thu March 2, 2017

POLITICS
## *Obama Strikes Back at Russia for Election Hacking*

By DAVID E. SANGER  DEC. 29, 2016

Americas                    Donald Trump | hacking | Russia
## Top US spy chief 'resolute' in belief Russia hacked US during election

US - Top spy chief 'resolute' in belief Russia hacke...

*Not an iota of evidence has been produced to back up the hysterical campaign alleging that Russia interfered in the election of President Trump.*

Russian hacking of Democratic Party emails to "Pearl Harbor," Japan's attack which brought the United States into World War II, and to "9/11." Russia has therefore, he claims, "attacked the core of our democracy."

But what was the actual content revealed in the first round of *Wikileaks*' publication of these emails? They exposed that the Democratic Party leadership had massively manipulated the electoral process in favor of Hillary Clinton and against Bernie Sanders. Second, *Wikileaks* published the speech Hillary Clinton gave before Wall Street bankers, in which she made it clear that, as President, she would represent Wall Street's interests. Robert Parry, the investigative journalist who won an unassailable reputation for his exposé of the Iran-Contra scandal, pointed out in his latest article ("The Policy Behind Russia-gate") that it hardly makes sense to call the leaks an attack on "the core of our democracy" if they helped the American people (as is their right) to be informed of these essential facts about a presidential candidate.

Just as the witch-hunt against Trump and several of his cabinet members and advisers reached a new high point, *Wikileaks* began to publish a new round of intelligence that surpasses the revelations of Edward Snowden. These revelations concern the total surveillance which—in addition to the NSA—the CIA (and the British intelligence service GCHQ) carries out throughout the entire world through tapping into smart-phones, tablets, computers, smart-TVs, and other electronic devices. This involves an unparalleled breach of the law, which has not yet led to a storm of outrage only because the frog is being cooked slowly, as the saying goes: The frog, thrown into cold water, doesn't notice that the temperature is slowly rising until it is too late. The CIA is strictly prohibited from carrying out operations within the United States against Americans. This time Mrs. Merkel has not even ventured her

RT video grab

*Robert Parry*

CC/Rama

*William Binney at the Congress on Privacy & Surveillance at the École Polytechnique Fédérale de Lausanne, on Sept. 30, 2013.*

pussyfooting statement that "Spying among friends—that is not acceptable."

But the revelation that the CIA has the technical capacity to *take control* of people's electronic devices and carry out hacking and other operations under a "false flag," was also part of the new *Wikileaks* release. That raises the legitimate question as to whether the alleged Russian hacking attacks may not have been carried out from CIA headquarters in Langley, Virginia—or perhaps from the U.S. consulate in Frankfurt, which has been identified as the secondary base of operations for CIA activities in Europe, China, and the Middle East. The very fact that letters of the Cyrillic alphabet and Russian names appeared in several of the hacking operations raises the question of "false flag" operations, since the most savvy hackers would hardly be so stupid as to leave their calling card on the tray.

These latest *Wikileaks* releases have turned the tide in the United States. The alleged links of the Trump team to Russia are no longer the only focus, but attention is now turned to the question of who is responsible for the illegal passing of information about the conversations of Trump associates with, for example, Russian Ambassador Sergey Kislyak, conversations that occurred in the reasonable pursuit of their functions as senators or members of the transition team. The Senate Judiciary Committee chaired by Sen. Charles Grassley, which is probing these questions, is now investigating in two directions—not only the alleged contacts of the Trump team with Russian institutions but, most notably, where the illegal leaks are coming from within the intelligence agencies.

Meanwhile, some former members of the intelligence community are speaking up, such as William Binney, one of the developers of the global NSA surveillance system—thus one of the top experts in this area and today a whistleblower like Edward Snowden—who condemn the

CIA's methods as absolutely unconstitutional. They say that these practices involve a total corruption of the legal system, that the United States is already a police state, and dangerously close to being a totalitarian state.

It may transpire that the alleged Russian hacking of the Democratic Party emails to help elect Trump was by no means a "Pearl Harbor" event, but that, on the contrary, Trump's friend of many years, Roger Stone, is right in his evaluation: Stone, who participated in many Republican election campaigns and administrations after serving as a member of the Nixon Administration, says that as an active witness of the scandals that ended Nixon's political career, this current affair is far more serious than Watergate. He says it constitutes the gravest breach of law and public morality in the history of the United States.

As for one of the questions that has now become relevant, as to who arranged for a request to the Foreign Intelligence Surveillance Court for authorization to surveil Trump, Stone stressed that it is improbable that it could have happened without Obama's agreement. In the Nixon case, the truth is that he didn't actually know in advance about the break-in at the Watergate Hotel, but despite that, he had to take responsibility for the crime. Today it is only a question of time as to when Obama, the former Secretary of Defense, and the heads of the CIA and FBI have to testify before a Grand Jury, and the whole issue could potentially become the greatest scandal in American history, Stone said. Very soon, the question will be: What did Obama know, and when did he know it?

## U.S., Russia, China Must Cooperate

The neoliberals and neoconservatives on both sides of the Atlantic are acting like children who shut their eyes and think that it makes them invisible. The whole world is talking about the bankruptcy of the working model of this Establishment, which thinks only of its own advantage, at the expense of the general welfare.

Donald Trump—who surely isn't perfect and must still demonstrate whether the trust placed in him was

Xinhua/Bao Dandan
*Chinese Foreign Minister Wang Yi speaking at the Center for Strategic and International Studies (CSIS) in Washington, D.C. on Feb. 25, 2016.*

justified, and in whose administration there lurk all kinds of potential submarines—was elected because a section of the American public that the neoliberal Establishment had written off, had had absolutely enough of endless wars, wars that had cost $6 trillion over 15 years, ruined countless soldiers and their families psychologically, and left them penniless; they had had enough of "rescue packages" for Wall Street, of the drug epidemic, of a life without a future.

The arrogant and pig-headed commentators in Europe should learn from the way that the strategic change is perceived in other parts of the world. On March 8—at his annual press conference at the National People's Congress—Chinese Foreign Minister Wang Yi stressed anew that China's objective is to stabilize the world situation through cooperation among the United States, Russia, and China, and thus promote worldwide economic, technological, and scientific development. The modern infrastructure projects that China has already initiated in 60 nations along the New Silk Road offer a platform for the most brilliant prospects for the whole world, if the most important nations participate. The New Silk Road initiative comes from China, he said, but it belongs to the whole world, and its success would benefit all nations.

It is admittedly difficult for people in Germany—who are faced with the totally lock-step mainstream media and their hysterical anti-Trump campaign, their demonization of Russian President Putin, and their ongoing negative reporting on China—to form a clear picture of what is happening in the world. But one thing should be clear to anyone who thinks it through: The world's problems can only be solved if the United States, Russia, and China cooperate. And only the political forces in Germany which are aligned with this perspective deserve to be supported.

Germany has a fantastic opportunity to bring its great cultural and scientific tradition into the shaping of the new paradigm of cooperation among all nations in win-win collaboration in the expansion of the New Silk Road. Don't let the "narratives" of the mass media block the way.

# Why the British Hate Trump

*The following is an edited transcript of remarks delivered by Michael Billington, an editor of Executive Intelligence Review, on the LaRouche PAC Webcast of March 10, 2017.*

**Michael Billington:** I thought I would make a presentation under the title, "Why the British Hate Trump." This is very important; Lyndon LaRouche has really emphasized that we're not going to win this unless people come to understand that we're dealing here with the British Empire. We always have been dealing with the British Empire. Many people thought LaRouche was either exaggerating or failed to recognize that the British Empire collapsed long ago. But now, it is very clear what he's been referring to for forty years or more, which is that we're dealing here with an America that has been largely taken over by the British Empire through Wall Street to some extent, but also through intelligence community operations and others. There is mounting proof for that. It is no longer the case that we're speaking in the darkness about the role of the British Empire. We're watching the evidence pour out, not only by implication, but in their own name. The British, in their own name, acknowledging that they are out to tear down the government of the United States, to carry out a coup against the democratically-elected government of the United States under Donald Trump.

## Britain's 'Get Trump Task Force'

There are many examples of this. I will mention a few, just to give you a flavor. The *Guardian* newspaper in London has now set up a website called "Resistance Now," which calls on all of those Americans disturbed by the horrible turn of events in America, who are out demonstrating, who are perhaps throwing Molotov cocktails, or feeding the press with stories about a Russian takeover of America to "please write in to our website, so we can compile all of this information for the betterment of people's knowledge of the horrors of Donald Trump."

Of course, this, to a certain extent, started with the release by MI-6 operative Christopher Steele of the 35-page notorious document full of absolutely crazy, made-up stories about how Donald Trump was being blackmailed by the Russians because they caught him cavorting with prostitutes, urinating on prostitutes, God knows what else. This Christopher Steele, an MI-6 operative, had been hired by the Democratic Party, the

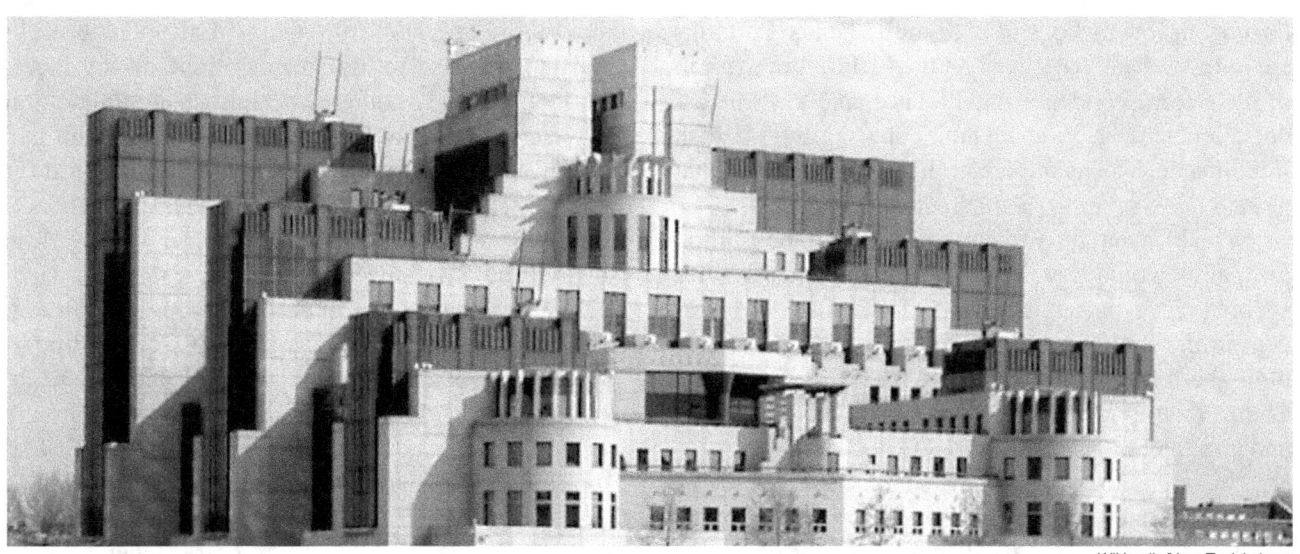

*The MI6 Building in London, 1994*

Obama/Hillary Clinton network, to carry out this fraud. The FBI then stepped in and wanted to continue the process, and actually offered to hire him on, and apparently did pay him for something we're not quite sure what. But this document was given to the FBI and to other intelligence agencies, and they acknowledged that there was absolutely no evidence for any of it. Nonetheless, they leaked it; it hit the press. This became the basis on which to launch this wild worse-than-McCarthy witch hunt coup attempt, based on the idea that it's not only wrong or improper, but outright illegal to have any contact with Russia, which is an absolutely absurd notion. As Trump himself has said many times, "it's a good thing to be friends with Russia, do you think we want a war? This would be a nuclear war, is that what you're promoting?" We have a situation now, where Steele is still being called, despite the discrediting of this nonsense, he's still potentially going to be testifying before the Congress. You have the same FBI which leaked this material to the press, saying quite openly that, in fact, we did get this material from the GCHQ, the Government Communications Headquarters which is the British NSA.

So, this is all public—it's not secret any longer. The British are doing their thing and we're going to get into why. Why do they hate Trump so much? I'll remind people that, on January 20th, we published an article by Helga Zepp-LaRouche in *EIR* called "The Foreign Power Corrupting US Politics Is London, Not Moscow," and that's now definitively demonstrated. We have some Congressmen who are taking this seriously. Senator Grassley, one of the most senior Senators, a Republican from Iowa who is head of the Judiciary Committee in the Senate, has called on the FBI to turn over all of their correspondence, intelligence, and any kind of documents they have about their connections to British Intelligence. This is important. I'm going to read what he said in his letter to [FBI Director] Comey:

"The idea that the FBI and associates of the Clinton campaign would pay Mr. Steele this [British] MI-6 agent "to investigate the Republican nominee for President in the run-up to the election, raises further questions about the FBI independence from politics, as well as the Obama administration's use of law enforcement and intelligence agencies for political ends."

This is serious. These are serious charges. Congressman Nunes, the Republican head of the House Intelligence Committee, has called for a hearing on March 20th which will have as witnesses James Comey of the FBI, Mike Rogers of the NSA, John Brennan of the CIA, and James Clapper, Director of National Intelligence. This is going to be quite interesting; we're looking here at treason. We're looking at a foreign government's collaboration with corrupted layers of the intelligence community to carry out a coup against our elected government. These are extremely serious, treasonous-style charges.

I'll mention one other thing. Suppose it were true, which it almost certainly is not, that the Russians had somehow been involved in the hacking of the DNC and the Podesta emails. First of all, this is not national security; these are private emails of a political party, not national security issues. Secondly, nobody's refuting that these are indeed the emails that showed that the Democratic Party was illegally, or at least against its own rules, manipulating the election to support Hillary Clinton against Bernie Sanders, and other serious irregularities. It's all true; nobody denies it. This is not fake news. This is real news. The fake news is that these [the leaks] are not being grabbed by journalists as an example of the democratic process, getting the truth to the American people. No, no; it's an intervention to destroy the democratic process by a foreign country, the Russians. It's ironic. It's insane, but it's ironic.

## The 'LaRouche Treatment'

Now I'll mention also that Lyndon LaRouche and our organization are quite familiar with this process. To a very real extent, Trump is getting the "LaRouche treatment." we know these corrupt layers of the FBI. We know how they connive with the British, because this was the operation run against LaRouche back in the 1980s that led to his incarceration and my incarceration, and that of others by the Bush administration for exactly the same reason. Lyndon LaRouche had put forward, and Reagan had adopted, his proposal for working with the Russians to end the Mutually Assured Destruction madness of Kissinger and the British: that the Russians and the Americans both have nuclear weapons aimed at each other ready to fire on the dropping of a dime, meaning that we won't go to nuclear war, because we know we'd get blown up, too. Of course, the point of this is that it keeps the world divided, and that's the intent of the British Empire. The core of this is to prevent the United States from working with Russia, prevent Europe from working with Russia, because the empire depends upon divide and conquer: Keep the world divided.

So, the same process, which was thrown against us for the same reasons, is now being thrown against Trump. And, as I think you know, we recently released a dossier on the third anniversary of the coup on the Maidan in Ukraine, where a neo-Nazi coup was openly backed by Obama and Soros and Obama's agent there, Victoria Nuland. This was a coup to put Nazis in power, run by Obama, Soros, and others, exactly those same individuals involved today in the operation to bring down the government of the United States, the Color Revolution against Trump. And again, it's for exactly the same reason. In both cases, this was to prevent collaboration between Europe and Russia, to prevent collaboration between the United States and Russia. Because this is the core of the Empire. It's really the same core group who maintain control over finances and trade on a global scale, by keeping people at war with each other so they don't object; nobody comes together to object to the imperial policy controlling global finance and trade.

I was basically getting at the fact that the coup against the United States is for that same reason. Because the ultimate division of the world by the Empire, uses ethnic divisions and religious divisions, and fighting over territories and things of this sort to keep people divided. But their big divide is East and West; the big divide is keep the democratic, free West and the still-dictatorial and communist East of Russia and China. Keep them separate at all costs. This is the basis on which we can prevent the coming together of nations which could once and for all end the very concept of empire.

Now, what is the concept of empire? It's divide and conquer, it's geopolitics versus win-win. This is true; but really it's more fundamental than that. It's basically a concept of man which is bestial in nature. It's a con-

*wikipedia*
*Charles Darwin maintained that humans were bestial, no different than animals: only the fittest survive.*

*public domain*
*For Darwinists, those people born to be strong must be capable of defeating the weaker people. A British officer getting a pedicure from his Indian servant in colonial India.*

cept of man which follows the Darwinian idea that humans are no different from the animals. Darwin's theory of how animals evolve is also false. He and his social Darwinist friends, Spencer and so forth, basically said this is the nature of man. This is the nature of human society, the survival of the fittest. Some people are born to be strong, and those strong people have to be capable of defeating the weaker people. Then they can survive in a world of one against all, an existentialist Hell of one against all. This is the core of the British Empire. they absolutely reject any concept that there can be common aims for mankind, that there can be a *win-win policy*, as Xi Jinping says, or a "common aims of mankind," as Helga LaRouche likes to call it. This is rejected. If you think about Darwin's ideas of evolution, it's obviously false, first of all, because it's based on the idea that things evolve by defeating somebody who threatens you.

## Human Development

But where does the evolution come from?—this is something that Mr. LaRouche has for many, many years addressed, using especially the Russian scientist Vernadsky. There's a lawfulness to the universe, which tends to move towards higher and higher concentrations of energy, energy-flux-density, which creates an environment in which higher order principles can take place, which led eventually to the emergence of life with chlorophyll. Then eventually in the same way, through positive evolution, not a negative survival of the fittest, to the emergence of animals and especially the emergence of human beings, capable of achieving a willful increase in relative population density based upon a higher capacity to organize the universe around certain principles. More importantly, when you reach the level of mankind, you're dealing here with a species capable of *escaping* from biological evolution. Escaping *entirely* from even what Darwin was looking at, because we, unlike animals, are not fixed, having to live within the confines of nature and the food that we have available to us. We have minds. We are capable of seeing the future, unlike animals, and we have the creative power to discover laws of the universe, which make it possible for us, then, to *organize* that universe to create conditions where we have higher and higher standards of living with greater population density, and so on.

This is what the British reject. Take, for instance, the argument of Malthus, another British genius, lunatic, genocidalist, who argues that there's a limit to human population because we're going to run out of resources. Well, we *never* run out of resources! Every discovery made by man, be it electricity by Ben Franklin, or radiation by the Curies, or nuclear reactions like Einstein discovered, each of these redefines what our resources are. The example that we've always used is that with fusion, seawater becomes a resource, and even better resources like helium-3 on the Moon, can fuel mankind practically forever. We redefine our existence. This is a *human* idea of man, as opposed to this British imperial *bestial* notion of man that justifies, not only between people but between *nations*, the right to have a slave system, an imperial system.

As I said, to return to the *political* side of this: the basic division of the British Empire, historically, has been this "East versus West" divide. Rudyard Kipling, one of the "geniuses" of the British imperial age, had the famous saying, that "East is East, and West is West, and never the twain shall meet." These are almost different species. Rudyard Kipling, in fact, *praised* the British Raj for "bringing civilization" to the Indians.

wikipedia

*Pastor Thomas Malthus maintained there was a limit to the Earth's human population because there was a limit to resources.*

Wikimedia commons

*By 1943, hordes of starving people were flooding into Calcutta, India, and many of them died. Churchill refused to send wheat, saying that they were "breeding like rabbits." According to Malthus, famine is nature's way of culling such "excessive" population.*

Recently, a new book was published by Shashi Tharoor. He's a very prominent personality, a Member of Parliament in India, a diplomat, a very educated fellow, who has been going after the British full tilt. He's just published a book called *Inglorious Empire: What the British Did to India.* He points out that in 1700, before the complete British takeover, India was the richest nation in the world. It had, according to him, 27% of the global GDP of the world; whereas the British had 1.8%. I don't know if that's true; I haven't read this book yet. But he does point out what I *do* know is true, which is that under the British, in one year, in 1837, 35 *million* people starved to death [in India], while the British were shipping wheat and other foodstuffs out of the country back to Britain. The British argument was "we don't interfere with famines, because famines are nature's expression of the limit of population. They had become overpopulated, and nature stepped in to cull the herd of the human beings. After all, we are moral people in the UK, and we believe in the morality of contracts. And to break a contract that sends the wheat back to the United Kingdom would be *absolutely immoral*, simply because 35 million people are starving to death." These are practically quotes. I'm not making this up. By the way, Tharoor also points out that 3.4 million people died under Winston Churchill. He compares Churchill to Adolf Hitler, a very apt comparison.

## Britain's Drug Empire

And then there's the Opium Wars; I don't need to go through it. These were wars by the British to literally destroy the Chinese government which was *opposing* the bringing in of opium from the Indian Raj to destroy the population of China in order to impose a similar kind of control.

Today, we see exactly the same thing. We can't think of these as dry history lessons. I meant to bring a copy of the book, *Dope, Inc.*, but I forgot—the book we published first in 1978 called *Dope, Inc.: The British Opium War Against America*. There have been several editions, the most recent is *Britain's Opium War Against the World*. The same banks that were set up in Hong Kong to run the opium wars—Hong Kong and Shanghai Bank, Standard and Chartered, the Jardine Matheson banks—these same banks are still at it today. When the HSBC was caught laundering tens of billions of dollars of drug money from Colombia and Mexico into the United States, the Obama administration said, "Nobody goes to jail. We're going to give them a slap on the hand, a little fine, and they can go back to work, running dope," because dope is the biggest business in the world. We've gone through on this show before a discussion about the fact that the head of the UN drug operation, [Executive Director of the United Nations Office on Drugs and Crime] Antonio Maria Costa, has made the point that in these crises periods, these banks *depended* upon the liquidity from the drug trade; in fact, all the time. It's the biggest business in the world.

As you know, while Obama was legalizing drugs across the United States, he was openly supporting both the national governments that were supporting drugs, as in Colombia, where they signed a so-called "peace agreement" with the FARC, which is nothing but a cocaine and marijuana cartel. Obama also made sure that the banks were allowed to continue unabated, because that's where the dope business actually is run.

Now we have Trump running a war on drugs, yet another reason the British absolutely hate Trump like they hated LaRouche. As you know, LaRouche started an organization called the Anti-Drug Coalition, publishing a magazine called *War on Drugs*. Trump has now declared a war on drugs. He's put a general, General John Kelly, in charge of Homeland Security, who is *intimately* familiar with the drug crisis, who has testified to the Congress that only 20 percent of the drugs coming across the Mexican border are caught at this point, and an Attorney General, Jeff Sessions, who has spent his whole life fighting against this legalization of drugs. This is not well-liked by the British, I can assure you.

Lastly, I'll mention what Jason is going to continue

with, which is that on the whole banking side of this, the British oligarchy *despise* the Hamiltonian system of credit. In an imperial system "money is dumb"; and that's what the British want people to be, is *dumb*. They want it to be based on money so that the banks control the flow of money; the money can be spent on whatever makes a profit, be it casinos or whorehouses—unlike the credit system set up by Alexander Hamilton and used by our best Presidents, credit which has a vision, which has an idea of the future, whose purpose is to create something, to create a better world, to actually look towards a future and make something change in a way which benefits the general welfare of the population.

This, I think, sort of rounds out a thumbnail sketch of the hell of the British Empire, why they hate Trump. Right now, perhaps for the first time in history, we are in a position where empire can be abolished, possibly forever, if we succeed in creating the kind of creative environment for the human race based on the common aims of mankind.

# Obama's 'Liberal' Killings in His War-for-War's-Sake in Afghanistan

by Ramtanu Maitra

March 11—Why are U.S. troops still killing and dying in Afghanistan, already the longest war in U.S. history? What are we achieving there? What possible outcome will ever allow them to return home—and when is it expected to happen? What have the deaths and maimings of Afghans, Americans and others achieved in sixteen years of war? All the broken families, all the heartaches—for what? And when will Barack Obama finally be made to answer these questions?

Prolonging an already six year-old war in Afghanistan and continuing it throughout his eight-year tenure by using deceptions, President Barack Obama has ended his years in the Oval Office with very little to show to the American people, other than a pile of dead bodies. Obama's "necessary war" in Afghanistan will not benefit the United States even an iota in the short or long run. All that Obama did during those eight years was to help kill more American soldiers and Afghans, civilians in particular, and leave behind a divided and increasingly ungovernable Afghanistan.

Seemingly, from the outset of his presidency, Obama adopted deception to hide his cold-blooded killer's instinct. For instance, "two days after taking the oath of office, Obama signed an Executive Order, which revoked the Bush-era directives authorizing torture, and re-emphasized international conventions and federal laws prohibiting torture. The following day, Obama authorized two Central Intelligence Agency drone strikes in northwest Pakistan, which, combined, killed an estimated one militant and ten civilians, including between

*Effects of a drone in Pakistan, neighboring Afghanistan.*

four and five children."[1] Obviously, these drone strikes violated all international conventions.

From the beginning, Obama was equally deceptive concerning troop strength in Afghanistan. In January 2009, soon after he moved into the White House, he wanted a review of the U.S. troop strength—but even before the review was completed, he sent 17,000 additional troops to Afghanistan, bringing the total to nearly 70,000 American troops on the ground.

During his eight years as commander-in-chief, Obama oversaw the deaths of 2,499 U.S. soldiers in Afghanistan and Iraq. Of those, 1,906 were killed in and around Afghanistan. That is about 75% of all U.S. soldiers killed since 2001. The International Committee of the Red Cross (ICRC) had 9,200 new patients in Af-

---

1. Micah Zenko, "Obama's Embrace of Drone Strikes Will Be a Lasting Legacy," *The New York Times,* Jan. 12, 2016.

ghanistan in 2015, and 1,261 were amputees. In addition, thousands have suffered crippling physical and mental injuries that have virtually destroyed their lives and killed their own and their family's dreams.

During his tenure at the White House, Obama conducted airstrikes on seven countries: Afghanistan, Iraq, Pakistan, Somalia, Yemen, Libya, and Syria. These airstrikes, and the war waged by Bush and Obama in Afghanistan with no discernable objective, have killed thousands of Afghan civilians. About 60% of these deaths were immediately caused by the enemy side of the Bush-Obama war, such as the Taliban.

DoD photo/Roland Balik, U.S. Air Force

*The remains of four U.S. Army members being transported to Dover Air Force Base, Del., Jan. 8, 2012.*

### Loss of Thousands of Lives

According to a July 2016 report by the United Nations Assistance Mission in Afghanistan (UNAMA), the total number of civilian casualties recorded by the UN between Jan. 1, 2009 and June 30, 2016, has risen to 63,934, including 22,941 deaths and 40,993 injured. Subsequently, the UN-reported civilian casualties in Afghanistan in 2016 were the highest ever recorded, with nearly 11,500 non-combatants—one-third of them children—killed or wounded. Fighting between Afghan security forces and armed groups, especially in populated areas, remained

U.S. Army/Sgt. 1st Class Michael J. Carden

*Marine Corps Cpl. Raymond Hennagir with the ball during training for the Warrior Games for wounded veterans at Walter Reed Army Medical Center in Washington, D.C., April 13, 2010.*

"the leading cause of civilian casualties" more than two years after NATO's combat mission ended, said UNAMA, which began documenting civilian casualties in 2009.[2]

It was evident at the beginning of 2009, when

Obama took charge of his "necessary war" in Afghanistan, that Washington had no clue who were its friends, who were its enemies, and what lies at the end of the killing in Afghanistan's mountains and valleys. Yet, Obama pushed forward with his killings, promising the American people that with the help of the U.S. and NATO troops, and his pro-active policy, the Washington-backed government in Kabul would be able to wrest control of the territories that were under the control of the Taliban. Did that happen? No, of course, it did not. The question is: Was it ever intended to happen?

In his Jan. 2017 report presented to the U.S. Congress, the Special Inspector General for Afghanistan Reconstruction (SIGAR), analyzing the high risks in Afghanistan, wrote: "Afghanistan needs a stable security environment to prevent it from again becoming a safe haven for al-Qaeda or other terrorists. More than half of all U.S. reconstruction dollars since 2002 have gone toward building, equipping, training, and sustain-

---

2. "Afghan civilian casualties at record high in 2016: UN," *Al Jazeera*, Feb. 6, 2017.

ing the Afghan National Defense and Security Forces (ANDSF). However, the ANDSF has not yet been capable of securing all of Afghanistan, and has lost territory to the insurgency. As of Aug. 28, 2016, U.S. Forces-Afghanistan (USFOR-A) reported that only 63.4% of the country's districts were under Afghan government control or influence, a reduction from the 72% as of Nov. 27, 2015." In fact, the Taliban controls more of the country now, than at any time since U.S. troops invaded in late 2001.

What was behind this failure? Is it because no one knew what was going on, or because some like Obama, and a few of his generals and CIA officials, believed that the United States and NATO can kill their way to subjugate the Afghans? Was that it?

DoD photo/Staff Sgt. Kaily Brown, U.S. Army.

*An Afghan National Army first sergeant on a patrol through a poppy field in Afghanistan, May 9, 2013.*

## Stuffing a Sink-Hole with Money

What is certain, however, is that there was no dearth of money going into the huge Afghan sink-hole created by the Bush and Obama administrations. During these sixteen years of war-for-war's-sake in Afghanistan, U.S. taxpayers threw in close to $800 billion, of which more than $600 billion was burned up during the 2009-2016 period. This amount also includes Coalition Support Funds for Pakistan. The U.S. Department of Defense describes the role of Coalition Support Funds as reimbursement for "expenses Pakistan incurs to conduct operations against al-Qaeda and Taliban forces including providing logistical support for its forces, manning observation posts along the Afghanistan border, and conducting maritime interdiction operations and combat air patrols."[3] That reimbursement adds up to about $15 billion.

In fact, the true cost of the Afghan war, like all other wars, was much more. Obama has dished out a few billions here, a few billions there to keep Pakistan as an ally in order to carry on his war-for-war's sake in Afghanistan. Much more importantly, this war has created thousands of injured veterans whom the American tax-

---

3. Office of the Under Secretary of Defense: Comptroller, *Overseas Contingency Operations, Operations and Maintenance, Defense-Wide,* 2015.

payers are obligated to take care of. When one adds up those expenses, we are staring at another trillion dollars over the years.

But that is not all the killings for which Obama can be credited. Another major killer that made its deadly appearance in the United States and elsewhere during the eight years of Obama, remains in the background, but it is as real as ever. It is the killing of even those younger than the soldiers, by opioids. Throughout Obama's reign in Washington, the Afghan poppy fields continued to bloom even more vigorously. Opium production spread almost throughout the country. The year Obama took over, opium production in Afghanistan had come down from its peak of 7,400 tons in 2007, to 4,000 tons in 2009. Since then, however, it has been rising again, and the 2016 production could be as high as that in 2007.

## Heroin, the Silent Killer

Between 2004 and 2009, as opium production jumped upwards, the Bush Administration decided to help with manual eradication. Some central Afghan units were trained by the U.S. contractor Dyncorp, as well as by regional governors and their forces—but the effort was not really designed to eradicate opium completely and hurt the cash-short big universal banks like HSBC, which launder the money. It was more of a jobs plan, and putting up a show for those who were concerned about the opium explosion. This futile effort saw about $7.6 billion salted away to make a few very rich, but, as expected, nothing else changed. In 2009, the Obama administration officially recognized that opium eradication had been a failure, and abandoned it altogether.

The claim by the Obama Administration that opium production was only helping the Taliban was never true. It helped the bankers who backed Obama for all eight years of his administration. It also created thousands of tons of heroin that affected young people across the world. As long as the Afghan heroin was moving north to affect millions of youths in Russia and Central Asia, Americans had no problem accepting the deceptions of the Obama Administration.

But things have changed in recent years. Now Americans have no choice but to be aware of the threat posed by heroin and other opioids. The monster that had caused such havoc elsewhere, is now killing off and debilitating young and not-so-young people right here in the United States. "In 2015, more than 52,000 Americans died of drug overdoses, according to the Centers for Disease Control and Prevention. That is an average of one death every ten minutes. Approximately 33,000 of these fatal overdoses—nearly two-thirds of them—were from opi-

creative commons

*A Taliban fighter.*

oids, including prescription painkillers and heroin. Although the absolute death toll from opioids is greatest in big cities like Chicago and Baltimore, the devastation is most concentrated in rural Appalachia, New England, and the Midwest. Many of the victims hail from white middle-class suburbs and rural towns."[4]

### The Surge to Kill

On Dec. 1, 2009, Obama, speaking at the United States Military Academy at West Point, New York, declared a surge in the U.S. troop strength in Afghanistan, and set the goal of "disrupting, dismantling, and defeating al-Qaeda and its extremist allies." On that occasion, he said: "Afghanistan is not lost, but for several years it has moved backwards. There's no imminent threat of the government being overthrown, but the Taliban has gained momentum. Al-Qaeda has not re-emerged in Afghanistan in the same numbers as before 9/11, but they retain their safe havens along the border. And our forces lack the full support they need to effectively train and partner with Afghan security forces and better secure the population. Our

---

4. "America's Opioid Epidemic is Worsening," *The Economist*, Mar. 6, 2017.

DoD photo/Lance Cpl. Justin M. Mason, U.S. Marine Corps

*U.S. Marines patrol on foot in Surobi, Afghanistan, May 23, 2004.*

*Afghan Taliban fighters.*

Al-Arabiya News Channel

new commander in Afghanistan—General McChrystal—has reported that the security situation is more serious than he anticipated." Obama said: "In short: The status quo is not sustainable," and following a full review, "as Commander-in-Chief, I have determined that it is in our vital national interest to send an additional 30,000 U.S. troops to Afghanistan. After eighteen months, our troops will begin to come home." At that time there were already 70,000 U.S. troops in Afghanistan.

Obama said that the additional 30,000 troops would tilt the situation in such a way that United States would be able to stabilize Afghanistan in eighteen months, after which the U.S. troops would start coming home. This observation was either based upon a supreme level of ignorance, or it was yet another deception with the intent to kill some more. What followed under his top Afghanistan war commander Gen. Stanley McChrystal, suggests that the latter was what was intended. In June 2010, Obama fired McChrystal, who was losing control of his troops. But Obama's killings continued under McChrystal's successor, Gen. David Petraeus.

American troop casualty figures in 2008 show there were 155 deaths. They shot up to 317 in 2009; 499 in 2010; 418 in 2011; and 312 in 2012, before Obama found his drones and the death figures began climbing down. In those years Afghan civilian casualties also rose sharply. According to the UN Assistance Mission in Afghanistan (UNAMA), 2,412 civilians were killed by the war in 2009, a jump of 14% over the number that lost their lives in 2008. An additional 3,566 Afghan civilians were wounded as a result of the war in 2009. UNAMA attributed two-thirds of the deaths to the action of anti-government forces.

In 2010, one of the deadliest years, UNAMA and the Afghanistan Independent Human Rights Commission (AIHRC) reported the deaths of 2,777 Afghan civilians, a jump of 15% over the civilian toll in 2009. Of these, UNAMA/AIHRC attributed 2,080 civilian deaths to insurgents, of which 55% were caused by suicide attacks and improvised explosive devices (IEDs)

In 2011, the United Nations reported that the civilian death toll numbered 3,021, a record high. In addition, 4,507 Afghans were wounded. The first half of 2011 was particularly deadly. 1,462 Afghan civilians were reportedly killed in the first six months of 2011, another 15% jump over the same period in 2010.

*Eight killed in U.S. drone attack in Pakistan in 2010.*

allpakistannews.com

U.S. Air Force/Staff Sgt. Lorie Jewell

*U.S. Army Gen. David H. Petraeus with Senator Barack Obama, on a tour of the Middle East and Europe, at Baghdad International Airport, Iraq, July 21, 2008.*

## Targeted Killings

In addition to the purposeless killing of the Afghans who opposed the Washington-directed government that alienated most Afghans, Obama and Petraeus went big with targeted killings. In a 2013 report, the London *Guardian* detailed the discussion of "kill lists" in the White House situation room with Obama in the chair. "Since the Obama Administration largely shut down the CIA's rendition program, choosing instead to dispose of its enemies in drone attacks, those individuals who are being nominated for killing have been discussed at a weekly counter-terrorism meeting at the White House situation room that has become known as Terror Tuesday. Barack Obama, in the chair and wishing to be seen as a restraining influence, agrees to the final schedule of names. Once details of these meetings began to emerge, it was not long before the media began talking of 'kill lists.' More doublespeak was required, it seemed, and before long the term 'disposition matrix' was born."[5] The disposition matrix "is a sophisticated grid, mounted upon a database that is said to have been more than two years in the development, containing biographies of individuals believed to pose a threat to U.S. interests, and their known or suspected locations, as well as a range of

options for their disposal," *Guardian* writer Ian Cobain explained.

On Sept. 2, 2010, the International Security Assistance Forces (ISAF), a combination of NATO and U.S. troops, announced that " 'coalition forces' had killed the Taliban deputy shadow governor of Takhar who was also a 'senior member' of the Islamic Movement of Uzbekistan (IMU) in an air attack. Immediately, Afghans, including the provincial governor, police chief, and President Karzai insisted an egregious mistake had been made, and civilians who had been campaigning in Afghanistan's parliamentary elections had been targeted. Ten were killed and seven injured."[6]

Subsequently, an investigation was launched at the behest of Afghan President Hamid Karzai. Kate Clark, analyzing the findings of this investigation, pointed out that "targeted killings—as one element of the so-called 'kill or capture' strategy—are one of the main metrics of success claimed by General Petraeus and an ever more important aspect of international military policy in Afghanistan. These operations are, in Petraeus's words, 'intelligence driven'. Yet, on the very day of the Takhar attack, he had voiced concerns to journalists about flaws in U.S. intelligence operations, in particular their lack of a 'granular understanding of local circumstances'."[7]

The Takhar incident was an outcome of the *modus operandi* adopted by Obama and his generals, particularly Gen. Petraeus. Afghanistan became the petri dish where the CIA and the Special Operations Forces (SOF) were combined to form a lethal, unaccountable paramilitary force which carried out their agenda outside of any overall military plan. "The vision floated in Washington this week was of an expanded and collaborative role for the SOF and CIA, as conventional forces withdraw. Admiral McRaven, a rising star since his Navy Seals killed Osama bin Laden in 2011, said that the Pentagon was considering handing more of the Afghan war responsibility over to a senior special operations officer and, in the same articles, it was said that an ap-

5. Ian Cobain, "Obama's Secret Kill List—The Disposition Matrix," *The Guardian,* July 14 2013.

6. Kate Clark, *The Takhar Attack,* Afghanistan Analysts Network, May 2011.

7. See footnote 6.

U.S. Army photo/Sgt. 1st Class Joe Belcher.

*Members of the Combined Joint Special Operations Task Force Afghanistan move through Torkham, Afghanistan with the 19th Special Forces Group, returning from a border meeting with Pakistani security officials, Feb. 10, 2004.*

pointment was expected in the summer."[8]

The involvement of the CIA and SOF in carrying out killings beyond the knowledge of the U.S. military sent out to "tame" the Taliban and eliminate al-Qaeda, raises questions. The CIA and SOF acted together in two areas: the CIA's operation of drones for targeting and killing and, along with the SOF, its potential command responsibilities over certain irregular Afghan armed groups.

As Clark pointed out, it is important to distinguish between civilians and the military. "The military helps protect civilians and encourages states to only grant the power to kill to trained military personnel with a transparent chain of command. All U.S. military personnel undergo training in the laws of armed conflict. All of those deploying to Afghanistan, get special training on preventing civilian casualties. The law is evident in military codes of conduct, training manuals, legal handbooks and some of the tactical directives. We do not know what training CIA agents might have before they use drones or work with Afghan armed groups. This very lack of transparency encourages breaches of the law and unaccounted-for killings."[9]

## Paramilitary Forces

By bringing the CIA and SOF into Afghanistan to carry out targeted killings, Obama also widened the fissures within Afghanistan. For instance, in October 2009, the *New York Times* said that Ahmed Wali Karzai, the brother of the Afghan president, was drawn into this network by the Obama Administration.

The ties to Mr. Karzai have created deep divisions within the Obama Administration. The critics say the ties complicate America's increasingly tense relationship with President Hamid Karzai, who has struggled to build sustained popularity among Afghans and has long been portrayed by the Taliban as an American puppet. The CIA's practices also suggest that the United States is not doing everything in its power to stamp out the lucrative Afghan drug trade, a major source of revenue for the Taliban.[10]

The article unveiled other operations that the Obama Administration was carrying out. It reported that Ahmed Wali Karzai was helping the CIA operate a paramilitary group, the Kandahar Strike Force (KSF). The KSF "is used for raids against suspected insurgents and terrorists. On at least one occasion, the strike force has been accused of mounting an unauthorized operation against an official of the Afghan government, the officials said."

The existence of the KSF, as well as the Afghan Guard Force, may be a secret in the United States, but not in Afghanistan. "Jules Cavendish of *The Independent*, who has doggedly followed such groups, has interviewed senior figures within the KSF, including their former leader, Atal Afghanzai. He described how KSF recruits were cherry-picked from regular Afghan army units and trained by U.S. SOF at Mullah Omar's old house, now known as Camp Gecko."[11]

8. Kate Clark, *War Without Accountability: The CIA, Special Forces and Plans for Afghanistan's Future*, Feb. 10, 2012.
9. See footnote 8.

10. Dexter Filkins, Mark Mazzetti and James Risen, "Brother of Afghan Leader Said to Be Paid by C.I.A.," *New York Times,* Oct. 28, 2009.
11. See footnote 8.

# Every Day Counts In Today's Showdown To Save Civilization

That's why you need EIR's **Daily Alert Service**, a strategic overview compiled with the input of Lyndon LaRouche, and delivered to your email 5 days a week.

The election of Donald Trump to the Presidency of the Untied States has launched a new global era whose character has yet to be determined. The Obama-Clinton drive toward confrontation with Russia has been disrupted--but what will come next?

Over the next weeks and months there will be a pitched battle to determine the course of the Trump Administration. Will it pursue policies of cooperation with Russia and China in the New Silk Road, as the President-Elect has given some signs of? Will it follow through against Wall Street with Glass-Steagall?

The opposition to these policies will be fierce. If there is to be a positive outcome to this battle, an informed citizenry must do its part--intervening, educating, inspiring. That's why you need the EIR Daily Alert more than ever.

---

**TUESDAY, NOVEMBER 22, 2016**

Volume 3, Number 65

### EIR Daily Alert Service

P.O. Box 17390, Washington, DC 20041-0390

- Only Global Solutions, Based on New Principles, Can Work
- Tulsi Gabbard Meets with Donald Trump Regarding Syria
- Robert Kagan Throws in the Towel, Complains U.S. Is Becoming 'Solipsistic'
- War Party Moving To Preempt Trump-Putin Reset
- Syrian Army Makes More Progress in Aleppo
- Duterte Gives OK to Nuclear Power for Philippines
- Europe Will Suffer from Maintaining Russia Sanctions
- Former Chilean Diplomat Confirmed, 'We Will Joyfully Welcome Xi Jinping'
- Duterte and Putin Establish Philippines-Russia Cooperation
- François Fillon, Pro-Russian Thatcherite, Wins First Round of French Right-Wing Presidential Primary

**EDITORIAL**

Only Global Solutions, Based on New Principles, Can Work

---

# III. An Aspect of LaRouche's Breakthrough

# Riemann Refutes Euler: Background to a Breakthrough

by Lyndon H. LaRouche, Jr.
October 18, 1995

**Editors' note:** *The magazine **21st Century Science & Technology** published, in its Winter 1995 edition, an English translation of a collection of early writings of Bernhard Riemann. We publish here Lyndon La-Rouche's introduction, "Riemann Refutes Euler," by permission of **21st Century**.*

In the following pages, *21st Century* presents the first known publication in English translation, of a group of posthumously published early writings of the famous physicist Bernhard Riemann (1826-1866).[1] These have the special significance of providing some relatively indispensable background for understanding how Riemann came to develop his earthshaking discoveries of 1853-1854.[2]

The special relevance of these pieces, pertains to the fact, that there can be no competent appraisal of Riemann's work, which does not treat his writings as, like those of Karl Weierstrass, a devastating refutation of Leonhard Euler's savage attacks on Gottfried Leibniz.[3]

The formal issue is the question, cloaked in a discussion of mathematical series, whether or not mathematical discontinuities exist.[4] The relevant substantive issue behind these attacks on Leibniz by the Eighteenth-Century newtonians, Dr. Samuel Clarke and Leonhard Euler, is, much more today than during Riemann's time, whether physics is a branch of mathematics, or mathematics a branch of physics.

As in the concluding sentence of his famous 1854 habilitation dissertation, Riemann demonstrated that, to settle the underlying issues of mathematics, one must depart that domain, into physics.[5] That statement plants Riemann, like his sponsor Karl Gauss before him, fully

1. See **Bernhard Riemann's Gesammelte Mathematische Werke**, Heinrich Weber, ed. (New York: Dover Publications reprint, 1953), "*Fragmente philosophischen Inhalts*," pp. 507-538. A more recent reprint of the same, Heinrich Weber's second edition (Stuttgart: B.G. Teubner, 1902), is Vaduz, Liechtenstein: Saendig Reprint Verlag Hans R. Wohlwend. Hereinafter, this is identified as **Riemann Werke**.
2. See Bernhard Riemann, "*Über die Hypothesen, welche der Geometrie zu Grunde liegen*" ("On the Hypotheses Which Underlie Geometry"), **Riemann Werke**, pp. 272-287. This is the famous June 10, 1854 habilitation dissertation, to which Albert Einstein referred, in identifying Riemann's work as a root of General Relativity. On the dating of the work embodied in this dissertation, 1853-1854, see H. Weber's reference to Riemann's note, which dates the discovery underlying the paper to "March 1, 1853": **Werke**, p. 508.
3. On Euler's attack on Leibniz, see Lyndon H. LaRouche, Jr., **The Science of Christian Economy** (Washington: Schiller Institute, 1991), Appendix XI, "Euler's Fallacies on the Subjects of Infinite Divisibility and Leibniz's Monads," pp. 407-425. That appendix includes the sections of Euler's **Letters to a German Princess** (dated by him May 5,

1761) in which his second explicit attack on Leibniz is made. The first occurred as his role in the scandalous case of Pierre-Louis Maupertuis, whose exposed fraud on the subject of "least action" led to Maupertuis's 1753 ouster from direction of the Berlin Academy; Euler was the principal accomplice of Maupertuis in perpetrating that hoax. We emphasize the primary coincidence between Riemann and Weierstrass here, not their secondary differences in approach.
4. See Leibniz-Clarke correspondence on the subject of the relationship between infinite series and the differential calculus. (G.W. Leibniz, **Philosophical Papers and Letters,** edited by Leroy E. Loemker, 2nd edition [Dordrecht: D. Reidel, 1969, reprinted Boston: Kluwer Academic, 1989], pp. 675-721.) Although Leibniz's development of the differential calculus had roots in some of his earlier activities, the archival evidence is, that what became known as Leibniz's calculus was actually developed during 1672-1676, in Paris, at Jean-Baptiste Colbert's Royal Academy of Science. Leibniz's first paper, presenting the discovery, was submitted for publication, in Paris, in 1676, immediately prior to his return to Germany. Isaac Newton's international reputation, and the Newton-Clarke attack on Leibniz, was created by Venice's Paris-based Abbot Antonio Conti (1677-1749), who sponsored a network of salons throughout Europe, a network devoted to the principal mission of seeking to discredit Leibniz, and build up Newton's reputation. Dr. Samuel Clarke was an agent of Conti, as were the Berlin circles of Maupertuis and Euler.
5. "*Es führt dies hinüber in das Gebiet einer andern Wissenschaft, in das Gebiet der Physik, welches wohl die Natur der heutigen Veranlassung nicht zu betreten erlaubt.*" ("This leads into the domain of another science, the realm of physics, which the nature of today's occasion does not permit us to enter.") Habilitation dissertation, **Riemann Werke**, p. 286.

*Bernhard Riemann (above) and Leonhard Euler (right). "Like Leibniz before him, Riemann's discovery demonstrates that formal mathematical-physics schemes do not embody the potentiality of a truth-doctrine. To find truth, we must depart the domain of mathematics, and go over into another domain, the realm of experimental physics."*

within the domain of physics, rather than the virtual reality which one associates with the influence of Bertrand Russell and the Bourbaki *Golem* upon much of today's teaching of mathematics. The posthumously published papers presented in English translation here, bear directly on Riemann's development of his approach to that issue.

## Riemann and Economics

*21st Century*'s attention to Riemann reflects my own original work in a branch of physical science founded by Leibniz, known as *physical economy*. My discoveries in this field supplied the principal impetus for the mid-1970s founding of the Fusion Energy Foundation, which ricocheted into the later founding of *21st Century* magazine. Although the principal part of my discoveries were not prompted by Riemann's work, the approach adopted for solving the mathematical problems posed by those discoveries was prompted almost entirely by Riemann's habilitation dissertation, leading to the designation of "LaRouche-Riemann Method."[6]

To introduce Riemann's posthumously published papers, I indicate the features of his dissertation which are most relevant to the problems of physical economy. To that end, consider, first, the place which mathematical discontinuities occupy in Riemann's discovery, and then, the significance of Riemann's emphasis on what he terms *Geistesmassen* in the posthumously published papers.

First, to define the significance of mathematical discontinuities, I restate Riemann's point of departure in his dissertation in my own words.

The origin of modern mathematics lies in what is commonly identified as a "Euclidean" notion of simple space-time. This idea of space-time pretends to represent the real universe, which it does not represent. It is an idea which is not a creation of the senses, but, rather, of the naive imagination. We merely imagine that space is defined by three senses of direction (backward-forward, up-down, side-to-side), and imagine that these might be extended without limit, and in perfectly uninterrupted continuity. We imagine that time is a single, limitless dimension of perfect continuity: backward-forward. Taken

6. See Lyndon H. LaRouche, Jr., "Why Most Nobel Prize Economists Are Quacks," **Executive Intelligence Review**, July 28, 1995, and

Lyndon H. LaRouche, Jr., "Non-Newtonian Mathematics for Economists," **Executive Intelligence Review**, Aug. 11, 1995.

together, these presumptions of the imagination define a four-dimensional space-time manifold, or, in other words, a quadruply-extended space-time manifold.

The naive imagination attempts to locate perceptible bodies and their motions within such a quadruply extended manifold. It may be said fairly, that our imaginary space-time manifold is used as a kind of mental mirror, upon which we attempt to project reflections of motion of bodies in space-time. The result of such projections is a simple "Euclidean" sort of algebraic mathematics, which, we soon discover, is not a mathematics of the real universe.

Classical experiments, typified by the measurement of the curvature of the Earth's surface by the ancient Eratosthenes of Plato's Academy at Athens,[7] supply measurable demonstration that the motion of bodies in physical space-time does not correspond to what a naive, algebraic notion of space-time suggests. We must add non-space-time "dimensions," such as the notions of "mass," "charge," and so forth, to derive a mathematics which agrees with our measurement of the motions which are reflected, from physical space-time, upon that imaginary mirror known as simple space-time.[8]

Thus, in place of a four-dimensional space-time of the imagination, the attempt to explore physical space-time presents us with a physical-space-time manifold of many more dimensions than the four dimensions of naive space-time. We call these added factors "dimensions," because they can be scaled, according to the ordering-principle of "greater than" and "less than," as we do the dimensions of naive space-time. Instead of saying $n+4$ dimensions, we include the four in our count of $n$; we speak, thus, of a "physical-space-time manifold of $n$ dimensions." Then, commonly, we attempt to portray motion within that physical-space-time, of $n$ dimensions, in terms of its imaginary reflection upon a four-fold space-time.

In each case, the addition of a validatable new "dimension" to the physical-space-time manifold of reference, corresponds to a change in measurement, a change in the yardstick we must employ to measure the relevant motion, or analogous form of action. For example, Eratosthenes estimated that the Earth was a spheroid of

about 7850 miles, from pole to pole (not a bad estimate for the time).[9] This meant, that to measure motion along the surface of the Earth, we must use a yardstick of spherical trigonometry, rather than one appropriate to a simple Euclidean plane. Similarly, once Ole Rømer had demonstrated, in 1676, that the radiation of light was governed by a principle of retarded potential, Christiaan Huygens, in 1677, generalized principles of reflection and refraction accordingly,[10] and, Jean Bernoulli and Leibniz demonstrated that the mathematics of the transcendental domain's special relativity must supersede the algebraic methods of Galileo, Descartes, and Newton.[11]

The validation of the necessary addition of such an added physical dimension, by measurement, implies the challenge to be considered here. Each such addition signifies, that instead of an $n$-fold physical-space-time manifold, $n$ is superseded by $(n+1)$. This gives us a generalized term of topology, which we might express symbolically by $(n+1)/n$. The series of changes, from $n$ to $n+1$ dimensions, is associated with a series of changes in the choice of the yardstick which we must employ to measure the relevant physical action.[12]

This is also the problem which confronts us, in physical economy, as one may attempt to define the correspondence between scientific and technological progress, on the one side, and, on the other side, a general, resulting increase in the productive powers of labor, per capita, per household, and per square kilometer. For that case, the type of yardstick used is termed *potential relative population-density*; that yardstick changes its scale (per capita, per square kilometer) as the level of applied scientific and technological progress advances.

## Science and Metaphor

All of the issues posed by Riemann's habilitation dissertation, while most profound, are so elementary that they might be understood at the level of a good secondary school's graduate. Once we accept his intention in that location, that paper is among the most lucid

7. See "How Eratosthenes Measured the Unseen" (Figure 2), in Lyndon H. LaRouche, Jr., "Kenneth Arrow Runs Out of Ideas, But Not Words," **21st Century,** Fall 1995, pp. 34-53.

8. This image is an accurate representation of the intent of Plato's reference to shadows which reality casts upon the imagination, as if these shadows were reflections on the wall of a cave's firelit interior.

9. **Greek Mathematical Works**, Ivor Thomas, trans., 2 vols. (Cambridge, Mass.: Harvard University Press, 1980), Vol. II, p. 273, note c.

10. Christiaan Huygens, **A Treatise on Light** (New York: Dover Publications reprint, 1962).

11. The "brachystochrone problem": Jean Bernoulli (1696). The equivalence of least time to least action.

12. This does not justify the presumptions of some popularized notions of a differential geometry. The basis for that word of warning will be made clearer below.

pieces of prose ever supplied to the literature of fundamental scientific discoveries. Admittedly, most of the classroom's putatively authoritative commentators have conveyed a contrary, confused view of this work. The failure of all such commentaries examined, is that the commentators, by refusing to accept the fact of what Riemann is saying, project upon him an intention which is axiomatically contrary to his own.

The axiomatic failures of such authoritative commentators occur on two levels.

Closer to the surface, they have sought to defend such post-1815 authorities in taught mathematics as Newton, Euler, Augustin Cauchy, et al. from the devastating refutation provided by Riemann's discovery. This centers around Euler's argument against Leibniz. That relatively more superficial axiomatic assertion, is the hysterical insistence of the positivists, that, ultimately, mathematical discontinuities do not exist.[13]

On the deeper level, there is a more devastating issue, which the opponents of Leibniz and Riemann refuse to debate.

The radical positivists of the Bourbaki cult exemplify this deeper issue. The peculiar, Ockhamite deism of such positivist ideologues, is the dogma, that all questions of science must be settled by mathematical proofs delivered upon a blackboard, or, by a modern digital-computer system. Every demonstration that mathematical formalism is not the god of science, whether by Plato and his academy after him, or from moderns such as Leibniz or Riemann, fills such positivists with an obscene, irrationalist rage, akin in spirit and rationality to that of Marat's or Danton's Jacobin mob.

This deeper of the two levels of axiomatic issues, underlies the assignment of Abbot Antonio Conti's agent, Dr. Samuel Clarke, for the attacks upon Leibniz. This is the issue underlying the savage, posthumous attacks upon Leibniz by the Conti salon's Euler. This was also the basis for the hyena-like attack, led by the devotees of Ernst Mach, upon Max Planck, during the period of World War I.[14]

Once we acknowledge the primary historical fact of mathematical-physical knowledge, that each of those discoveries of physical principle which is validated by the appropriate measurement, presents mathematics with a topological challenge of the indicated $(n+1)/n$ form, mathematical formalism is stripped of that attributed, god-like authority which the devotees of Euler and the Bourbaki cult defend so fanatically.[15] Like Leibniz before him, Riemann's discovery demonstrates that formal mathematical-physics schemes do not embody the potentiality of a truth-doctrine. To find truth, we must depart the domain of mathematics, and go over into another domain, the realm of experimental physics.

The key to all among these, and derived formal issues of mathematical physics, is the connection between the erroneous insistence, that, ultimately, no discontinuities exist in mathematics, and the deeper assumption (also false), as among the followers of the Bourbaki dogma, that mathematics can be a truth-doctrine.

It is admissible to state, that any consistent mathematical physics of a specific, $n$-fold physical-space-time manifold, can be read as if it were a formal, deductive theorem-lattice. In this interpretation, it appears that every theorem of that lattice has the qualifying attribute of being a proposition which has been shown to be not-inconsistent with whatever set of axioms and postulates underlie that lattice in its entirety.[16] Such a set of axioms and postulates is identified by both Plato and Riemann as an *hypothesis*, in contrast to the illiterate's misuse of the same term in Newton's famous "*et hypotheses non fingo.*"[17]

The literate usage of "hypothesis," is mandatory in reading even the title of Riemann's June 1854 dissertation, even before proceeding to the body of the text. The key to a literate reading of Riemann's dissertation, is that a topological transformation typified by the transition from a mathematically $n$-fold physical-space-time

13. Formally, Euler's assertion was a defense of the purely arbitrary assumption of the naive Euclidean imagination, that linear extension is perfectly continuous without limit. Since Euler's supposed proof of that assertion depends absolutely upon the assertion of that axiom which it purports to prove, Euler's famous tautology proves nothing at all. Euler's folly on this point is the hereditary origin, via Lagrange and Laplace, of Cauchy's bowdlerization of Gottfried Leibniz's version of a calculus.

14. That attack upon Planck, first from within the German-speaking scientific community of the World War I interval, was continued in the savagery of Niels Bohr and other accomplices of Bertrand Russell, during the period of the famous 1920s Solvay Conference sessions.

15. This is literally an ancient issue. This topological challenge is the same ontological paradox, of the "One" and "Many," posed by Plato's **Parmenides**.

16. E.g.: What Euler defends, by means of a rather silly tautology, in his 1761 attack upon Leibniz, is the naive, Euclidean, axiomatic assumption of the perfect persistence of linearization indefinitely, into the very large and very small.

17. **Riemann Werke**, p. 525: "*Das Wort Hypothese hat jetzt eine etwas andere Bedeutung als bei Newton. Man pflegt jetzt unter Hypothese Alles zu Erscheinungen Hinzugedachte zu verstehen.*"

manifold, to a manifold of (*n*+1) dimensions, is a transformation in the set of axioms and postulates underlying mathematical physics.

Consequently, the history of those discoveries of physical principle which, like Eratosthenes' discovery of an estimated curvature of the Earth, are validated by the relevant measurement, presents us with a succession of topological changes within mathematical physics, a series of changes which has the form of the "One"/"Many" paradox of Plato's **Parmenides.** In this instance, the "Many" are represented by a series of hypotheses; the challenge is to discover a higher principle, an *higher hypothesis*, a "One," which defines a generative principle by means of which the series of hypotheses, the "Many," is ordered "transfinitely." If Riemann's dissertation is read in any different sense than this platonic one, the resulting commentary upon the text is a scientifically illiterate one, no matter what the putative classroom authority of the commentator.

Riemann adopts a view of mathematical physics based upon the succession of advances in those discoveries of physical principle which have been validated crucially by relevant measurement, such as Eratosthenes' estimate for curvature of the Earth typifies that principle of measurement. Riemann's view of this topological transformation underlying mathematical physics' progress, thus defines progress in mathematical physics in terms of a sequence of absolute mathematical discontinuities within a formalist reading of mathematical physics itself. It defines Newton, Euler, and Cauchy, for example, as victims of their own scientific illiteracy, victims of an ontological paradox, of the "One/Many" form, which they could neither solve, nor comprehend—and, apparently, did not wish to comprehend.

In each case, one formal theorem-lattice is distinguished from another by any change in the axiomatic content, from that of the hypothesis underlying one, to that of the hypothesis underlying the other; every theorem of the second lattice is formally inconsistent with any theorem of the first. The difference between the two hypotheses, is a true, and relatively absolute mathematical discontinuity. Such a "discontinuity" has the same significance in mathematical physics as the proper understanding of the term "metaphor" in Classical forms of poetry or drama. What "discontinuity" signifies respecting the formalities of a consistent mathematical physics, is precisely what "metaphor" signifies for a Classical poem or drama.[18] The understanding of this relationship between metaphor and mathematical discontinuity, is the key to the first of the posthumously published documents, "On Psychology & Metaphysics," presented in the following pages.

In physics, a mathematical discontinuity appears as a mere mark. The magnitude of this mark is of *transinfinitesimal* smallness, so small that no calculable arithmetic magnitude can measure it, yet it exists, nonetheless, as a phenomenon: apparently as a mark of separation of all magnitudes which are less, from all magnitudes which are greater.[19] This mark signifies the functional presence, outside the realm of mathematical formalities, of the mathematical-physical form of what we recognize in Classical poetry as a metaphor.

## Riemann's 'Geistesmassen'

The fact that all true metaphors are singularities, is the key to an accurate understanding of Riemann's use of *Geistesmassen*, translated here as "thought masses," in the first of the posthumously published papers, "On Psychology and Metaphysics." As an illustration of the principle involved, consider the case of metaphor in either a Classical form of strophic poem, or a song-setting of such a poem by a Mozart,[20] Beethoven, Schubert, Schumann, or Brahms.[21] This case, of the Classical

---

18. The relevant problem is that, many miseducated readers with advanced degrees in arts have the same difficulty in coping with the term "metaphor," which radical positivists experience with the term "mathematical discontinuity." Beginning the early Seventeenth Century, the empiricists, such as Thomas Hobbes, launched a vile, energetic, and persisting campaign to eradicate the use of metaphor and the subjunctive mood from English-language usage. The recent emergence of that radical-existentialist decadence known as the "deconstructionism" of Professor Jacques Derrida, et al., is the outgrowth of a centuries-long campaign by the empiricists and logical positivists, and related linguistics specialists, to locate the origin of written language, even Classical poetry, in "text" as such, rather than the irony-rich domain of speech.

19. In the extremely small, discontinuities are compared in respect to their mathematical cardinality, not as arithmetic values. Hence, with deference to Georg Cantor, this distinction is designated here by the usage of "transinfinitesimally small."

20. After Mozart's first song composed in the new mode of motivic thorough-composition, his setting of Johann Goethe's "Das Veilchen" ("The Violet"). See A Manual on the Rudiments of Tuning and Registration, John Sigerson and Kathy Wolfe, eds. (Washington: Schiller Institute, 1992), Chapter 11, pp. 199-228.

21. Op. cit., pp. 220-221. Note the reference to Gustav Jenner, **Johannes Brahms als Mensch, Lehrer und Künstler: Studien und Erlebnisse** (Marburg an der Lahn: N.G. Elwert'sche Verlagsbuchhandlung, 1930). Jenner's account of Brahms' instruction to him on composing a song for a strophic poem, is directly relevant to the point being developed at this point in the text, above.

strophic poem, and its musical setting according to principles of motivic thorough-composition, is key for understanding the mental processes by means of which a validatable discovery of new scientific principle is generated.[22] This is also an example of the conception posed by Plato's treatment of the "One/Many" ontological paradox in his **Parmenides** and other late dialogues.[23]

In the successful Classical poem, efficiently illustrated as to form by Goethe's simple **Mailied**,[24] the strophes represent a succession of metaphors, which march, one after the other, toward a conclusion. The metaphorical attribution of each of those strophes is generated by ironies, to such effect that no proper attribution of either a confining literal or a symbolic meaning for that strophe is to be permitted. The concluding metaphor, especially its final couplet, changes radically the metaphorical attribution—e.g., the "meaning"—of the poem as a whole. It is that concluding, subsuming metaphor, which identifies the idea of the poem taken in its entirety.

The literate reading of such a poem, or its Classical song-setting, demands a repeated review of the completed poem, until the point is reached that two conditions are satisfied: first, that the idea of the completed poem as a whole is clear; second, that the relationship of each step of progress within the poem, to the reaching of the conclusion, is clear.[25] The satisfaction of that requirement establishes the idea of the poem as a whole, in the mind, as the product of a tension between two, literally platonic qualities of idea. The first, is the idea of the completed poem in its entirety; this idea remains unchanged, from prior to the re-reading of the first line, to the momentary silence following the reading of the last line. The second idea, is the successive metamorphoses which the idea of the poem undergoes, in proceeding from the beginning to the end. In Plato, that latter quality of idea is identified as the *Becoming*. It is the tension between the fixed conception, the idea of the completed poem as a whole, and the metamorphical character of the process of Becoming, by which the perfected idea is reached, which is the "energy" of the poem.

The same requirement applies to the performance of any Classical musical composition. In the simplest case of such a musical performance, it is the performer's memory of reaching the perfected (completed) composition, which creates the tension of reenacting the performance of the metamorphosis, the tension between the perfected idea of the composition, and the moment of development in mid-performance.

The singularity in question is generated by the difference in direction of time-sense—backwards versus forwards—of the two, interacting ideas respecting the poem or musical composition in mid-performance.

The same principle characterizes Eratosthenes' estimate of the curvature of the Earth's surface: the principle of development uncovered, by re-experiencing the mutually contradictory individual readings of the midday sundials, to locate a generating principle of change which is consistent with the final result. For Eratosthenes, the key to the generating principle becomes the relationship between the perimeter of a circle and a pencil of lines, from a momentarily fixed position of the point corresponding to the Sun, to the Earth. Thus, Eratosthenes gave a reasonable estimation of the Earth's curvature, approximately twenty-two centuries before any person saw that curvature.

These examples, from poetry, music, and the work of Plato's Academy of Athens, are each and all examples of *platonic ideas*, the quality of ideas to which Riemann assigns the term *Geistesmassen*. In physical science generally, such ideas have initially the apparent character of ideas arising from vicious inconsistencies within observations made by aid of sense-perception, inconsistencies which mock both naive sense-certainty and generally accepted scientific opinion. Relatively often, that mockery occurs in the most cruelly devastating way. Those ideas which purport to identify the generating principle responsible for this paradox, and which are validated by relevant modes of measurement, represent valid discoveries of physical principle. Those qualities of proven principle are classically identified as *platonic ideas*. Each and all of the validated ideas of "dimensionality" in an *n*-fold physical-space-time manifold, have this quality of platonic idea.

Thus, all such ideas have the form of paradoxical

22. See Lyndon H. LaRouche, Jr., "Musical Memory and Thorough-Composition," **Executive Intelligence Review**, Sept. 1, 1995, pp. 50-63.

23. Plato's **Parmenides** is to be considered as a kind of prefatory piece for all of his later dialogues. In it, he poses the challenge, the ontological paradox, which is the subject addressed in its various aspects by all of the other late dialogues.

24. LaRouche, "Musical Memory and Thorough-Composition," p. 55. See note 22.

25. See Jenner's account of his instructions from Brahms, on memorizing a poem with sufficient thoroughness to satisfy those requirements, before undertaking to provide a song-setting for it. See note 21.

singularities relative to the pre-existing mathematical domain of reference. The character of these ideas as singularities arises from the way in which their existence is generated *subjectively*: by the same kind of processes underlying the reading and composition of a valid Classical strophic poem. The quality of "singularity," and the associated form of mathematical discontinuity, arises from the opposing senses of time associated with the interplay of perfected ideas with the process of their development.[26]

These metaphors can never be deduced from the mathematics, or other form of language employed. Within the language itself, they appear merely in the reflected form of singularities, such as either mathematical discontinuities or other paradoxical adumbrations reflected into the language-medium. The ontological existence of the singularity lies outside the form of generation of the relevant mark within the domain of the language itself.

Thus, every theorem which claims to deny the existence of discontinuities within mathematics, such as Euler's, is based upon *the tautological fallacy of composition, of using constructions premised axiomatically on linearization, to prove the utterly irrelevant point, that any construction of this type is incapable of acknowledging any mathematical existence which is not linear!*

The relevant formal mathematical discontinuity, or literary paradox, is merely the mark which the metaphor imposes, as its footprint, upon the formally defined medium of language. The actual metaphor, which the adumbrated mark, or paradox reflects, exists only outside the medium. It lies within three locations. It lies, first, in the substance of the process which the language is attempting to describe. It also lies, secondly, in the mental processes of the scientist, or the artist. It exists, thirdly, within the sovreign mental processes of those members of the audience who have responded Socratically to the mark of the singularity, by generating in their own mind a replication of the idea which has imposed its mark upon the medium of communication.

In mathematical physics, the validation of the ideas corresponding to such marks occurs commonly through measurements which demonstrate, that those ideas correspond efficiently to an effect which is not in correspondence with the old ideas which the new ideas profess to supersede.

There is a most notable illustration of this point in the case of Riemann's paper, published in 1860, "On the Propagation of Plane Air Waves of Finite Amplitude."[27] The fact that acceleration toward speeds above the speed of sound generates a singularity, was recognized by Riemann as showing the existence of the transsonic phenomena studied by such followers as Ludwig Prandtl and Adolf Busemann. It was this principle of Riemann's which resulted, through the mediation of a German aerospace specialist, in the first successful powered, post-World War II, supersonic flight by a U.S. aircraft. This was in contrast to the failed contrary opinion expressed by such frequent adversaries of Riemann's work as Hermann Helmholtz, Lord Rayleigh, and Theodor von Karman.[28]

In the relatively more obvious type of case, such as the cited Eratosthenes case, the empirical validation of such a singularity is accomplished by measurements which lie within the domain of arithmetic magnitudes. However, this is not the only primary form of empirical proof of a platonic idea. As Riemann's referenced paper on shock-waves illustrates the point, in some cases, it is the existence of a non-arithmetic singularity, which has precise cardinality, but not arithmetic magnitude, which presents us the mathematical form of the required proof. Riemann's success in forecasting a class of phenomena not necessarily limited to this cited case, not only pow-

---

26. The proper notions of topology are derived from this consideration.

27. "*Über die Fortpflanzung ebener Luftwellen von endlicher Schwingungsweite*," **Riemann Werke**, pp. 156-175. This was published in an English translation by Uwe Henke and Steven Bardwell, in the Fusion Energy Foundation's **International Journal of Fusion Energy**, Vol. 2, No. 3, 1980, pp. 1-23.

28. There is a relevant story behind the Fusion Energy Foundation's publication of that translation. During the middle to late 1970s, the Fusion Energy Foundation (FEF) gained an international reputation for its important work in promoting inertial confinement fusion. As a consequence of this, in 1978, two representatives of the FEF, Mr. Charles B. Stevens, Jr., and Dr. Steven Bardwell, were invited to the Soviet Union to participate in an international scientific conference on inertial confinement. Prior to their departure, these two FEF representatives met with LaRouche and others, at a Bronx location, to obtain LaRouche's list of requirements for that Moscow visit. LaRouche requested that they ask Soviet scientists for unclassified documents pertaining to the use of Riemann's work on isentropic compression as a basis for the original development of thermonuclear ignition. Such unclassified documentation was obtained, identifying this Riemann *Fortpflanzung* paper in that connection. It was at a subsequent, "report back" meeting that same year, that LaRouche underlined the application of the same paper to physical-economic modelling, and presented the set of inequalities used to create the highly successful 1980-1983 U.S. Quarterly Economic Forecast of the **Executive Intelligence Review (EIR)** newsweekly.

ered transsonic/supersonic flight, but isentropic compression in thermonuclear ignition, is an example of this.

## Leibniz's Universal Characteristic

Respecting the ontological implications of metaphor itself, within these posthumously published pieces, Riemann picks up on a theme addressed earlier by Leibniz, and later revived by the present writer. We must consider the fact, that those efficient platonic ideas recognizable as validated discoveries of principle, are generated as discoveries within those sovreign mental processes of the individual which are impenetrable by symbolic communications-media, such as a formal mathematics. Yet, despite the ethereal quality one might be tempted to attribute wrongly to such mental processes, the result of such ideas is an increase of the human species' physical power to command nature in general.

In this respect, these papers of Riemann turn our attention back to Leibniz's notion of a *Universal Characteristic*, which subsumes, commonly, non-living, living, and cognitive processes within our universe. This is the topical area addressed in the first two of the posthumously published papers: "I. On Psychology and Metaphysics," and "II. Epistemological issues." After the writing of these papers, Riemann's published work does not refer explicitly again to such epistemological underpinnings of science. From 1854 on, his published work limits itself essentially to mathematical physics, with some impingement upon biophysics,[29] although he clearly did not abandon that personal standpoint in his thinking about mathematical-physics matters. Therein lies some of the special importance of the posthumously published papers for identifying the deeper implications of Riemann's work as a whole.

My own discoveries in physical-economy were rooted in my youthful profession as a follower of Leibniz, and in my developing a rigorous defense of Leibniz against Immanuel Kant's attacks upon him, the latter a matter which bears directly upon the issue of Leibniz's notion of a Universal Characteristic. Furthermore, my discoveries were provoked by both the positivist excesses of Norbert Wiener's "information theory" and the similar incompetence of the work in systems analy-

sis by one of Wiener's followers, John von Neumann; these positivist concoctions I had treated as parodies of Kant's attack on Leibniz. For this reason, my rereading of Riemann brought to that reading the same emphasis upon Leibniz's Universal Characteristic which we encounter in the first two items among Riemann's posthumously published pieces.

The kernel of Wiener's hoax in "information theory," was to adopt and misuse a term, "negative entropy," which had been used earlier chiefly to identify the qualitative distinction between living and non-living processes as they present themselves on the scale of macrophysics.[30]

In successful modern physical economies, my field of study, the biological appearance of "negative entropy" is echoed by the requirement that the ratio of relative "free energy" to "energy of the system" must not decrease, despite the accompanying requirement of rising per-capita and per-square-kilometer values of capital-intensity and power-intensity. This desired result is realized, typically, by the fostering of increase of the (physical) productive powers of labor through investment in scientific and technological progress.

Consider the following summary of the relevant argument elaborated in other locations.[31]

Physical economy identifies the primary phenomena of economic processes in terms of market-baskets of both necessary physical consumption and certain crucial classes of services, limited essentially (in modern society) to education, health care, and science and technology as such. These market-baskets are defined per capita (of labor-force), per household, and per square kilometer of relevant land-area employed. The market-baskets are defined for personal consumption, for the processes of production, and for those improvements in land-area used which we class under

---

29. E.g., the brilliantly confirmed analysis provided within his *Mechanik des Ohres* (Mechanics of the Ear): **Riemann Werke**, pp. 338-350.

30. As noted, repeatedly, in other locations, this reporter has found it desirable to apportion all physical science among four functionally distinguished domains of inquiry. Two areas, astrophysics and microphysics, are domains in which the scale of phenomena is either too large, or too small, to be addressed directly by the senses. In a third area, biophysics, we deal with the principled distinction between processes, such as organic compounds, which, in one instant are functioning as part of a living process, and, in another instant, not. This also defies simple sense-perception. Those three domains, leave, as residue, the domain of macrophysics, in which sense-perception plays a larger immediate role.

31. E.g., Lyndon H. LaRouche, Jr., "Why Most Nobel Prize Economists Are Quacks," and "Non-Newtonian Mathematics for Economists." See note 6.

"basic economic infrastructure." Physical economy recognizes a required functional relationship between the level of these market-baskets and the productive powers of labor, as measured in terms of both production and consumption of the content of these market-baskets.[32]

That yields an implied differential expression: What level of input (consumption) is required to maintain a certain rate of output of necessary products for consumption? Without yet knowing the exact answer to that question at any given point, the idea of the question is clear. This idea is expressed conveniently as the notion of *potential relative population-density*.[33]

The levels of combined market-basket consumption which are required to maintain not less than some constant rate of potential relative population-density, are compared to the notion of "energy of the system." Output of market-basket content in excess of those required levels, is compared to "free energy." The "free energy" is considered "not wasted," on the condition that it is consumed in market-basket forms, for both expanding the scale of the economy, and increasing the potential relative population-density. It the latter case, the capital-intensity ("energy of the system" per capita, per household, and per square kilometer) must increase, and the power-density must also increase. The requirement is, that the ratio of apparent "free energy" to "energy of the system" must not decrease, despite a rising relative value of "energy of the system" per capita, per household, and per square kilometer.

The increase of potential relative population-density, under the condition that those constraints are satisfied, is treated as the economic-process analog for what is expressed as "negative-entropic" evolutionary self-development of the biosphere in biology and in the terms of reference supplied by the Academician V.I. Vernadsky's notion of biogeochemistry. To avoid confusion with the "information theory's" popularized misuse of the term "negative entropy," the term "not-entropy" is employed instead.

In the field of what Academician V.I. Vernadsky defined as biogeochemistry, this requires the evolution of the biosphere, to bring the entire system to a higher state of organization; Vernadsky's argument typifies the line of thought which is otherwise encountered in various locations, including Leibniz's notion of a Universal Characteristic, and also the referenced portions of Riemann's posthumously published papers.

Wiener made a mess of everything, with the popularization of his wretched insistence that "negative entropy," for which he employed the neologism "negentropy," was no more than a reversal of the statistical entropy described by Ludwig Boltzmann's H-theorem. Contrary to Wiener's mechanistic schemes, if we account for mankind and mankind's activity as part of the planetary system, man's increased power over nature, typified by the increase of mankind's potential relative population-density,[34] is actually an increase of the relative "negative entropy," or, "not-entropy," of the planetary system as a whole. In other words, mankind's development supplies an evolutionary upward impulse to the totality of the system with which mankind interacts.

In this view of the matter, human cognition has developed within the domain of living processes, but those ecological characteristics of the human species which are entirely due to cognition, place mankind absolutely apart from and above all other living species. Thus, our universe subsumes the interaction among three distinguishable types of processes: non-living, living, and cognitive. The commonly subsuming principle governing such a universe, is Leibniz's notion of a Universal Characteristic.

For today's conventional classroom opinion, what we have just stated poses the question: "Is it not necessarily the case, that if the 'not-entropy' of society increases, that this must occur at the price of increasing the entropy of the universe with which society is interacting?" In other words, is the relationship of society to the remainder of the universe not what von Neumann's devotees term "a zero-sum game"? The crux of the issue, is that the idea of "universal entropy" is not a product of scientific discovery, but of the reckless application of an axiomatically linear, mechanistic worldview, upon the interpretation of the evidence of kinematic models of gases; on this account, there is an

---

32. E.g., the case for household consumption was indicated by Gottfried Leibniz in **Society and Economy** (1671), which appears in English translation in **Executive Intelligence Review**, Jan. 4, 1991, pp. 12-13.

33. On "relative population-density," see Lyndon H. LaRouche, Jr., **So, You Wish to Learn All About Economics?** (New York: New Benjamin Franklin House, 1984). This introductory textbook has been published in various languages, including Russian, Ukrainian, and, most recently, Armenian.

34. Per capita of labor-force, per household, and per square kilometer of relevant land-area employed.

amusing ambiguity in the ironical meaning Norbert Wiener's work supplies to the term "gas theory."

The absurdity of the popular version of doctrines of "universal law of entropy," is suggested by the fact, that every rational effort to describe the universe in the large, is an evolutionary model, in which development is vectored as progress to relatively higher states of organization. In mathematical terms, this progress to higher states of organization is indicated by the emergence of physical systems whose characteristics can not be identified without resort to the mathematics of successively higher cardinalities. The attempt to explain the efficient directedness of such universalizing processes of emergence of higher cardinalities, renders absurd every attempt to explain the existence of matter itself in terms of a mechanistic dogma of "building blocks." The evidence is, that recognizably higher physical states of cardinality, are accomplished by transformations of the entire system, not by accretions of objects of a mechanistically fixed domain.

The counterposing of the developmental (e.g., not-entropic) and Kant-like mechanistic views is noted by Riemann, in the first of the referenced papers. Crucial is the demonstration, that, as in the case of Euler's absurd 1761 attack on Leibniz's **Monadology**, the presumption of that Kant-like, mechanistic view, from which Richard Clausius, Lord Kelvin, and Hermann Grassmann concocted their chimerical "Second Law of Thermodynamics,"[35] is "axiomatic linearization in the small." Create a mathematics, in which all is subsumed under the axiomatic assumption, that everything in the universe is consistent with the Euclidean blind faith in the universality of perfectly continuous linear extension, even into the extremely great and the extremely small. The true believer then regards any formulation which is inconsistent with such a mathematical "proof," as "disproven," and everything which must be assumed to preserve consistency within the theorem-lattice of such a mathematics, is considered as "proven" by all of the awesomely credulous professorial, head-nodding dupes attending the relevant conference.[36]

Once we recognize, that such a mathematics constitutes no proof at all respecting the issues immediately at hand, the most generous consideration which the advocates of the "Second Law" might require of rational people, is the famous Scots' verdict, "not proven." No axiom of a mathematics is proven by the employment of the formal mathematical theorem-lattice whose existence depends upon that included assumption.

Those qualifying observations stated, situate the matter at hand. Now, turn directly to the subject of Leibniz's Universal Characteristic.

The paradigmatic form of all increase in mankind's potential relative population-density, from the several millions potential of a man-like higher ape, to the billions of today, is changes in social-productive behavior typified by general application of the fruits of scientific and technological progress.[37]

Each of the transmitted discoveries is known by means of the replication of that original act of discovery within the mind of the hearer. On the condition that education of the young proceeds according to that latter principle, present-day knowledge is the accumulation of all of those singularities which valid past discoveries

---

35. It was Kelvin who proposed to Clausius this radically mechanistic interpretation of Sadi Carnot's work. In this case, as in all of his attacks upon Bernhard Riemann, Clausius relied upon Hermann Grassmann for the mathematical side of his endeavors. See **Riemann Werke**, note on page 293. The crucial role which the axiomatic presumption of linearization in the small played in Grassmann's work, including all of his work on the "Second Law" and attacks upon Riemann, is reflected in his famous 1844 work founding a relevant branch of modern vector analysis, the so-called *Ausdehnungslehre*.

36. During 1978, former FEF Director Morris Levitt dug out a document authored by J. Clerk Maxwell which caused FEF much amusement at that time. In this document, Maxwell responded to the question: Why had Maxwell failed to give credit to such predecessors as Wilhelm Weber and Riemann (and also, most crucially, the founder of electrodynamics, Ampère) for many of the discoveries which Maxwell tacitly presented as either the work of Michael Faraday, or his own? To this, Maxwell replied, that "we," referring to the circles including Kelvin, et al., had chosen to disregard any work which relied upon geometries "different than our own." The same point is made, in similar terms, in Maxwell's principal work. The implication of Lord Rayleigh's denunciation of Riemann's *Fortpflanzung* paper, is the same: the root of the mechanistic world-view, which the empiricist world-outlook of modern Britain acquired from its ancient master, Paolo Sarpi, is always the presumption of the universality of percussive causality within a universe which is axiomatically linearized in the very small.

37. This progress in the human condition is not due only to scientific and technological progress. The metaphors which arise from Classical forms of poetry, tragedy, and music have as crucial a role in increasing man's power to exist as what we term conventionally "natural science." Nonetheless, as we have already indicated, valid fundamental scientific discoveries merely typify the more general case for all forms of expression of the creative-mental powers of persons as metaphor: as the great English poet Percy Shelley expressed the point, within his "A Defence of Poetry": the "power of communicating and receiving intense and impassioned conceptions respecting man and nature." What is stated above, here, should be read with the understanding that the case for scientific ideas *typifies* the case for metaphor in general.

have conveyed to the use of the present generations: just as students today would be scientific illiterates, until they re-experience the original discoveries by the members of Plato's Academy at Athens in this way, from Plato, Eudoxus, and Theaetetus, through Eratosthenes. Without a Classical education of the young, in the great Classical works of poetry, tragedy, music, and natural science, going back to the foundations of modern civilization over 2,500 years ago, there can not be a truly civilized or even rational society, a cruel fact we see enacted so brutishly on our streets and in our government and universities today.

Each valid such discovery invokes the principle we have associated here with the topological symbol $(n+1)/n$. Each discovery is a singularity of that type. Progress in knowledge is an accumulation of such singularities. As Riemann emphasizes, within the texts provided below, that accumulation of knowledge is interactive, every new concept interacting with every other accumulated within the same mind. Thus, with every thought, this increase of singularities is reflected efficiently: in mathematical terms, the density of discontinuities for any arbitrarily selected interval of human action, is increased. It is this increase of "density of discontinuities" which typifies the form of "not-entropic" and the form of the action which generates "not-entropy" in, for example, the form of increase of society's potential relative population-density.

The crucial fact is, that this increase of knowledge, as defined in this way, is consistently efficient. *The universe obeys the human creative-mental powers' command! Thus, as* **Genesis 1** prescribes, mankind exerts dominion over nature. Conversely, the universe is manifestly so constituted, that it is prone to submit to the authority of that power of creative reason which is a potentiality peculiar to the individual human personality.

By accumulating a reliving of the original valid acts of discovery of principle, which constitute the accumulation of human knowledge to the present date, we are enabled to recognize the distinguishing features of that form of act of creative reason, by means of which valid discoveries have been commonly achieved. That experience becomes known to us, as to Johannes Kepler, as *Reason*, or, as for Gottfried Leibniz, as *necessary and sufficient reason*. Once we recognize, that mankind's cumulative development of knowledge represents the power of the human will to command the universe according to the law embedded in that universe, we have shown ourselves that *reason* as we define it *subjectively* in this way, is also an efficient approximation of Reason as it exists, ostensibly *objectively*, as an efficient principle pervading the universe as a whole.

What we recognize in the form of "not-entropy," as in the increase of society's potential relative population-density, is the characteristic of Reason, both as it exists efficiently, "objectively" within the universe at large, and as we are able to adduce the principles of reason, "subjectively," through the efficiency of valid discoveries of principle in the domains of science and art.

Once that is acknowledged, then it is clear to us, that the universe is not linearized in the extremely small, or extremely large. It is "not-entropic," in the extremely small and extremely large, alike. To see this more clearly, it was sufficient, to shift the emphasis in reading Riemann's contributions to mathematical physics, away from physics narrowly conceived, back to the vantage-point of Leibniz, the vantage-point of physical economy, the vantage-point of the efficient relationship between valid human individual reason, and man's increased power over the universe. Thus, we may say, that not-entropy, as reflected in type by Riemann's topological expression $(n+1)/n$, corresponds to what Leibniz named a Universal Characteristic.

# EDITORIAL

### IT IS EHRICKE'S POLYGLOBAL WORLD

# A New System of International Relations Emerges Everywhere on the Planet

by Kesha Rogers

March 13—A new system of international relations is now emerging everywhere on this planet. We are truly embarking on a New Paradigm for all mankind. This new paradigm can been understood through the beautiful expression of State Councilor Yang Jiechi of China, in his description of the upcoming Belt and Road Forum for International Cooperation, to be held on May 14-15: "The Belt and Road Initiative was proposed by China. Yet it is not going to be China's solo show," Yang said, adding that "A better analogy would be that of a symphony performed by an orchestra composed of all participating countries." As UN General Assembly President Peter Thomson of Fiji expressed it, in referring to the New Silk Road in a recent interview with Xinhua, Xi's vision "is the only future for humanity on this planet."

One can also say that the related vision of the great German-American space pioneer and rocket scientist, Krafft Ehricke, is the only future for humanity, on and off this planet! It is coherent with President Xi's vision. We should celebrate Ehricke's upcoming 100th birthday, just a few days from now, on March 24.

Just as China today speaks of a multipolar world, and a system of win-win cooperation through the development of the Belt and Road Initiative (the New Silk Road), and the development of space infrastructure platforms for the mutual benefit of all nations, Ehricke similarly envisioned what he called an "open-world" system, a world of unlimited growth, and expansion throughout the universe. Ehricke called it a polyglobal world. A world not bounded by so-called "limited resources" in which we believe that we are "running out of everything," or the "closed-system" of geopolitics, in which mankind is limited to one small planet.

The development of a permanent lunar colony is key to mankind's expansion throughout the Solar system. How will this be accomplished? Not by priva-

*Krafft Ehricke with space station model, April 17, 1958.*

*State Councilor of China Yang Jiechi*

Widmann/MSC

We must make sure that our government immediately takes up these policies. We must restore our national mission for physical economic development, including space exploration and colonization, for the benefit, and with the cooperation of all nations, and in fulfillment of what Ehricke, the great space pioneer and aeronautical engineer, called "Mankind's Extraterrestrial Imperative."

A *permanent manned lunar presence* can only be realized through the vision of lunar development outlined by Ehricke, most emphatically in his 1984 report titled," Lunar Industrialization and Settlement—Birth of Polyglobal Civilization." In this work he writes,

tized, commercial spaceflight and "public-private partnerships" for so-called cheap tourist flights to the lunar surface and other planetary bodies. The achievement of a permanent lunar presence is the gateway to the development of a human economy in space. And that requires the creation of a new system of economic value, not defined in monetary terms, but using national credit to fund those great projects that will "provide for the general welfare" of our Nation, as referenced in the Preamble to our Constitution.

The realization of such a goal requires the immediate implementation of Lyndon LaRouche's Four Laws, starting with the immediate reinstatement of Franklin Roosevelt's original Glass-Steagall Act. Second, a new National Bank must be created. Third, this new national credit must be directed into energy-dense projects in the productive economy, new technologies, and infrastructure platforms. Finally, crash programs must be adopted to finally achieve thermonuclear fusion technologies and restore an energetic, imaginative, and purposeful space program. (See the video, https://www. youtube.com/watch?v=vKD20EjUYi4)

LaRouche develops his entire Four Laws platform around the principle he defines as "the essential distinction of man from all lower forms of life." Recognizing this distinction, he says, the Four Laws platform "presents the means for the perfection of the specifically affirmative aims and needs of human individual and social life." Advances in human creativity and productive capacity are key, not money!

Our work in space will change Earth's present closed-world environment into an open one with access to vast space resources and other critically needed benefits that will greatly improve the lives of all people, and preserve Earth at it's best—as man's home and garden for the maximum human future.

This makes very clear Ehricke's understanding that space travel and exploration are not for cheap thrills and billionaire fantasies, but are absolutely essential to new scientific discoveries and economic platforms, needed for the advance of human civilization.

Ehricke outlines five essential stages of lunar development. He recognized the Moon as an essential proving ground for our development in space:

The Moon is the logical proving ground for subsequent industrial developments and settlements elsewhere. Only 2-3 flight days away, it allows us to develop, at our very doorstep, the experience we need to operate successfully and cost-effectively in more distant regions. No other celestial body and no orbiting space station can more effectively permit development of the habitats, material extraction and processing methods, and in essence, all the science, technology, and sociology required for a responsible approach to extraterrestrial operations.

Ehricke's five stages of lunar development are these: First, we examine the Moon from Earth. Second, we examine the Moon from lunar orbit, consider what might be the optimal site for an industrial base, and establish automated laboratories and pilot facilities on the surface. Third, we locate the best spot on the Moon for an initial industrial base, and establish it there. Fourth, from this base we establish a larger industrial zone that can return resources to Earth while expanding around the Moon. And fifth, we expand and diversify from this base to create a translunar space-faring civilization, a civilization that has gone beyond the Moon to other bodies.

These five stages of lunar development are centered on the growth of what Ehricke calls the "human sector":

> The most important aspect of lunar development lies in the human sector. It bears repeating that technological progress and environmental expansion are no substitutes for human growth and maturity, but they can help the human reach higher maturity and wisdom.

This is the outlook and perspective that any U.S. President requires in defining a serious national mission for space exploration and development. This is what is required for a permanent lunar colony and cooperation among nations in the creation of a truly "polyglobal," "open-world" system. The United States must reject the existing, failed economic paradigm and join in the "win-win" paradigm offered through cooperation with China and Russia. President Trump's meeting with China's President Xi on April 6 could be the beginning of a new relation between the two nations and the opening for the United States to join in cooperation with China and many nations at the upcoming Beijing Belt and Road Summit. Our national mission for space exploration and development must be based on a vision of cooperation in scientific and technological advance for the common aims and the peace of all mankind.

Krafft Ehricke reminds us of Mankind's Extraterrestrial Imperative:

> Space opens new horizons beyond Earth and offers new beginnings in ways we can manage this precious planet. It offers noble aspirations, opportunities for creative action, for bringing the human family closer together and contributing to a better future for all.

Let us proceed, as indeed we must!